Thoughtful Machine Learning with Python

A Test-Driven Approach

Matthew Kirk

Beijing · Boston · Farnham · Sebastopol · Tokyo

Thoughtful Machine Learning with Python

by Matthew Kirk

Printed in the United States of America.

Published by O'Reilly Media, Inc., 1005 Gravenstein Highway North, Sebastopol, CA 95472.

O'Reilly books may be purchased for educational, business, or sales promotional use. Online editions are also available for most titles (*http://oreilly.com/safari*). For more information, contact our corporate/institutional sales department: 800-998-9938 or *corporate@oreilly.com*.

Editors: Mike Loukides and Shannon Cutt
Production Editor: Nicholas Adams
Copyeditor: James Fraleigh
Proofreader: Charles Roumeliotis

Indexer: Wendy Catalano
Interior Designer: David Futato
Cover Designer: Randy Comer
Illustrator: Rebecca Demarest

January 2017:   First Edition

Revision History for the First Edition
2017-01-10:   First Release
2017-10-20:   Second Release

See *http://oreilly.com/catalog/errata.csp?isbn=9781491924136* for release details.

978-1-491-92413-6

[LSI]

Table of Contents

Preface

I wrote the first edition of *Thoughtful Machine Learning* out of frustration over my coworkers' lack of discipline. Back in 2009 I was working on lots of machine learning projects and found that as soon as we introduced support vector machines, neural nets, or anything else, all of a sudden common coding practice just went out the window.

Thoughtful Machine Learning was my response. At the time I was writing 100% of my code in Ruby and wrote this book for that language. Well, as you can imagine, that was a tough challenge, and I'm excited to present a new edition of this book rewritten for Python. I have gone through most of the chapters, changed the examples, and made it much more up to date and useful for people who will write machine learning code. I hope you enjoy it.

As I stated in the first edition, my door is always open. If you want to talk to me for any reason, feel free to drop me a line at *matt@matthewkirk.com*. And if you ever make it to Seattle, I would love to meet you over coffee.

Conventions Used in This Book

The following typographical conventions are used in this book:

Italic
: Indicates new terms, URLs, email addresses, filenames, and file extensions.

`Constant width`
: Used for program listings, as well as within paragraphs to refer to program elements such as variable or function names, databases, data types, environment variables, statements, and keywords.

`Constant width bold`
: Shows commands or other text that should be typed literally by the user.

Constant width italic

Shows text that should be replaced with user-supplied values or by values determined by context.

This element signifies a general note.

Using Code Examples

Supplemental material (code examples, exercises, etc.) is available for download at *http://github.com/thoughtfulml/examples-in-python*.

This book is here to help you get your job done. In general, if example code is offered with this book, you may use it in your programs and documentation. You do not need to contact us for permission unless you're reproducing a significant portion of the code. For example, writing a program that uses several chunks of code from this book does not require permission. Selling or distributing a CD-ROM of examples from O'Reilly books does require permission. Answering a question by citing this book and quoting example code does not require permission. Incorporating a significant amount of example code from this book into your product's documentation does require permission.

We appreciate, but do not require, attribution. An attribution usually includes the title, author, publisher, and ISBN. For example: "*Thoughtful Machine Learning with Python* by Matthew Kirk (O'Reilly). Copyright 2017 Matthew Kirk, 978-1-491-92413-6."

If you feel your use of code examples falls outside fair use or the permission given above, feel free to contact us at *permissions@oreilly.com*.

O'Reilly Safari

Safari (formerly Safari Books Online) is a membership-based training and reference platform for enterprise, government, educators, and individuals.

Members have access to thousands of books, training videos, Learning Paths, interactive tutorials, and curated playlists from over 250 publishers, including O'Reilly Media, Harvard Business Review, Prentice Hall Professional, Addison-Wesley Professional, Microsoft Press, Sams, Que, Peachpit Press, Adobe, Focal Press, Cisco Press, John Wiley & Sons, Syngress, Morgan Kaufmann, IBM Redbooks, Packt, Adobe

Press, FT Press, Apress, Manning, New Riders, McGraw-Hill, Jones & Bartlett, and Course Technology, among others.

For more information, please visit *http://oreilly.com/safari.*

How to Contact Us

Please address comments and questions concerning this book to the publisher:

O'Reilly Media, Inc.
1005 Gravenstein Highway North
Sebastopol, CA 95472
800-998-9938 (in the United States or Canada)
707-829-0515 (international or local)
707-829-0104 (fax)

We have a web page for this book, where we list errata, examples, and any additional information. You can access this page at *http://bit.ly/thoughtful-machine-learning-with-python.*

To comment or ask technical questions about this book, send email to *bookquestions@oreilly.com.*

For more information about our books, courses, conferences, and news, see our website at *http://www.oreilly.com.*

Find us on Facebook: *http://facebook.com/oreilly*

Follow us on Twitter: *http://twitter.com/oreillymedia*

Watch us on YouTube: *http://www.youtube.com/oreillymedia*

Acknowledgments

I've waited over a year to finish this book. My diagnosis of testicular cancer and the sudden death of my dad forced me take a step back and reflect before I could come to grips with writing again. Even though it took longer than I estimated, I'm quite pleased with the result.

I am grateful for the support I received in writing this book: everybody who helped me at O'Reilly and with writing the book. Shannon Cutt, my editor, who was a rock and consistently uplifting. Liz Rush, the sole technical reviewer who was able to make it through the process with me. Stephen Elston, who gave helpful feedback. Mike Loukides, for humoring my idea and letting it grow into two published books. Alexey Porotnikov who helped me extensively with the Python coding examples.

I also want to give special thanks to Alexey Porotnikov (*https://github.com/alpo*) who painstakingly helped me convert all these examples from Ruby to Python and also from Python 2 to Python 3. Seriously, thank you!

I'm grateful for friends, most especially Curtis Fanta. We've known each other since we were five. Thank you for always making time for me (and never being deterred by my busy schedule).

To my family. For my nieces Zoe and Darby, for their curiosity and awe. To my brother Jake, for entertaining me with new music and movies. To my mom Carol, for letting me discover the answers, and advising me to take physics (even though I never have). You all mean so much to me.

To the Le family, for treating me like one of their own. Thanks to Liliana for the Lego dates, and Sayone and Alyssa for being bright spirits in my life. For Martin and Han for their continual support and love. To Thanh (Dad) and Kim (Mom) for feeding me more food than I probably should have, and for giving me multimeters and books on opamps. Thanks for being a part of my life.

To my grandma, who kept asking when she was going to see the cover. You're always pushing me to achieve, be it through Boy Scouts or owning a business. Thank you for always being there.

To Sophia, my wife. A year ago, we were in a hospital room while I was pumped full of painkillers…and we survived. You've been the most constant pillar of my adult life. Whenever I take on a big hairy audacious goal (like writing a book), you always put your needs aside and make sure I'm well taken care of. You mean the world to me.

Last, to my dad. I miss your visits and our camping trips to the woods. I wish you were here to share this with me, but I cherish the time we did have together. This book is for you.

## CHAPTER 1

Probably Approximately Correct Software

If you've ever flown on an airplane, you have participated in one of the safest forms of travel in the world. The odds of being killed in an airplane are 1 in 29.4 million (*http://www.statisticbrain.com/airplane-crash-statistics/*), meaning that you could decide to become an airline pilot, and throughout a 40-year career, never once be in a crash. Those odds are staggering considering just how complex airplanes really are. But it wasn't always that way.

The year 2014 was bad for aviation; there were 824 aviation-related deaths (*http://bit.ly/2014-aviation*), including the Malaysia Air plane that went missing. In 1929 there were 257 casualties (*http://bit.ly/casualties-1929*). This makes it seem like we've become worse at aviation until you realize that in the US alone there are over 10 million flights per year, whereas in 1929 there were substantially fewer—about 50,000 to 100,000. This means that the overall probability of being killed in a plane wreck from 1929 to 2014 has plummeted from 0.25% to 0.00824%.

Plane travel changed over the years and so has software development. While in 1929 software development as we know it didn't exist, over the course of 85 years we have built and failed many software projects.

Recent examples include software projects like the launch of healthcare.gov, which was a fiscal disaster, costing around $634 million dollars (*http://bit.ly/cost-healthcaregov*). Even worse are software projects that have other disastrous bugs. In 2013 NASDAQ shut down due to a software glitch and was fined $10 million USD (*http://reut.rs/2i2HfgS*). The year 2014 saw the Heartbleed bug infection, which made many sites using SSL vulnerable. As a result, CloudFlare revoked more than 100,000 SSL certificates, which they have said will cost them millions (*http://bit.ly/cost-heartbleed*).

Software and airplanes share one common thread: they're both complex and when they fail, they fail catastrophically and publically. Airlines have been able to ensure safe travel and decrease the probability of airline disasters by over 96%. Unfortunately we cannot say the same about software, which grows ever more complex. Catastrophic bugs strike with regularity, wasting billions of dollars.

Why is it that airlines have become so safe and software so buggy?

Writing Software Right

Between 1929 and 2014 airplanes have become more complex, bigger, and faster. But with that growth also came more regulation from the FAA and international bodies as well as a culture of checklists among pilots.

While computer technology and hardware have rapidly changed, the software that runs it hasn't. We still use mostly procedural and object-oriented code that doesn't take full advantage of parallel computation. But programmers have made good strides toward coming up with guidelines for writing software and creating a culture of testing. These have led to the adoption of SOLID and TDD. SOLID is a set of principles that guide us to write better code, and TDD is either test-driven design or test-driven development. We will talk about these two mental models as they relate to writing the right software and talk about software-centric refactoring.

SOLID

SOLID is a framework that helps design better object-oriented code. In the same ways that the FAA defines what an airline or airplane *should* do, SOLID tells us how software *should* be created. Violations of FAA regulations occasionally happen and can range from disastrous to minute. The same is true with SOLID. These principles sometimes make a huge difference but most of the time are just guidelines. SOLID was introduced by Robert Martin as the Five Principles. The impetus was to write better code that is maintainable, understandable, and stable. Michael Feathers came up with the mnemonic device *SOLID* to remember them.

SOLID stands for:

- Single Responsibility Principle (SRP)
- Open/Closed Principle (OCP)
- Liskov Substitution Principle (LSP)
- Interface Segregation Principle (ISP)
- Dependency Inversion Principle (DIP)

Single Responsibility Principle

The SRP has become one of the most prevalent parts of writing good object-oriented code. The reason is that single responsibility defines simple classes or objects. The same mentality can be applied to functional programming with pure functions. But the idea is all about simplicity. Have a piece of software do one thing and only one thing. A good example of an SRP violation is a multi-tool (Figure 1-1). They do just about everything but unfortunately are only useful in a pinch.

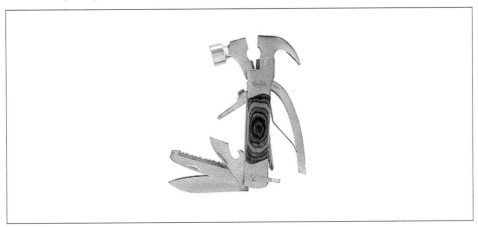

Figure 1-1. A multi-tool like this has too many responsibilities

Open/Closed Principle

The OCP, sometimes also called encapsulation, is the principle that objects should be open for extending but not for modification. This can be shown in the case of a counter object that has an internal count associated with it. The object has the methods increment and decrement. This object should not allow anybody to change the internal count unless it follows the defined API, but it can be extended (e.g., to notify someone of a count change by an object like Notifier).

Liskov Substitution Principle

The LSP states that any subtype should be easily substituted out from underneath a object tree without side effect. For instance, a model car could be substituted for a real car.

Interface Segregation Principle

The ISP is the principle that having many client-specific interfaces is better than a general interface for all clients. This principle is about simplifying the interchange of data between entities. A good example would be separating garbage, compost, and recycling. Instead of having one big garbage can it has three, specific to the garbage type.

Dependency Inversion Principle

The DIP is a principle that guides us to depend on abstractions, not concretions. What this is saying is that we should build a layer or inheritance tree of objects. The example Robert Martin explains in his original paper[1] is that we should have a `Key boardReader` inherit from a general `Reader` object instead of being everything in one class. This also aligns well with what Arthur Riel said in *Object Oriented Design Heuristics* about avoiding *god classes*. While you could solder a wire directly from a guitar to an amplifier, it most likely would be inefficient and not sound very good.

 The SOLID framework has stood the test of time and has shown up in many books by Martin and Feathers, as well as appearing in Sandi Metz's book *Practical Object-Oriented Design in Ruby* (*http://poodr.info*). This framework is meant to be a guideline but also to remind us of the simple things so that when we're writing code we write the best we can. These guidelines help write architectually correct software.

Testing or TDD

In the early days of aviation, pilots didn't use checklists to test whether their airplane was ready for takeoff. In the book *The Right Stuff* by Tom Wolfe, most of the original test pilots like Chuck Yeager would go by feel and their own ability to manage the complexities of the craft. This also led to a quarter of test pilots being killed in action.[2]

Today, things are different. Before taking off, pilots go through a set of checks. Some of these checks can seem arduous, like introducing yourself by name to the other crewmembers. But imagine if you find yourself in a tailspin and need to notify someone of a problem immediately. If you didn't know their name it'd be hard to communicate.

The same is true for good software. Having a set of systematic checks, running regularly, to test whether our software is working properly or not is what makes software operate consistently.

In the early days of software, most tests were done after writing the original software (see also the waterfall model (*https://en.wikipedia.org/wiki/Waterfall_model*), used by NASA and other organizations to design software and test it for production). This

---

1 Robert Martin, "The Dependency Inversion Principle," *http://bit.ly/the-DIP*.

2 Atul Gawande, *The Checklist Manifesto* (New York: Metropolitan Books), p. 161.

worked well with the style of project management common then. Similar to how airplanes are still built, software used to be designed first, written according to specs, and then tested before delivery to the customer. But because technology has a short shelf life, this method of testing could take months or even years. This led to the Agile Manifesto (*http://agilemanifesto.org*) as well as the culture of testing and TDD, spearheaded by Kent Beck, Ward Cunningham, and many others.

The idea of test-driven development is simple: write a test to record what you want to achieve, test to make sure the test fails first, write the code to fix the test, and then, after it passes, fix your code to fit in with the SOLID guidelines. While many people argue that this adds time to the development cycle, it drastically reduces bug deficiencies in code and improves its stability as it operates in production.[3]

Airplanes, with their low tolerance for failure, mostly operate the same way. Before a pilot flies the Boeing 787 they have spent X amount of hours in a flight simulator understanding and testing their knowledge of the plane. Before planes take off they are tested, and during the flight they are tested again. Modern software development is very much the same way. We test our knowledge by writing tests before deploying it, as well as when something is deployed (by monitoring).

But this still leaves one problem: the reality that since not everything stays the same, writing a test doesn't make good code. David Heinemer Hanson, in his viral presentation about test-driven damage (*http://bit.ly/test-induced-damage*), has made some very good points about how following TDD and SOLID blindly will yield complicated code. Most of his points have to do with needless complication due to extracting out every piece of code into different classes, or writing code to be testable and not readable. But I would argue that this is where the last factor in writing software right comes in: refactoring.

Refactoring

Refactoring is one of the hardest programming practices to explain to nonprogrammers, who don't get to see what is underneath the surface. When you fly on a plane you are seeing only 20% of what makes the plane fly. Underneath all of the pieces of aluminum and titanium are intricate electrical systems that power emergency lighting in case anything fails during flight, plumbing, trusses engineered to be light and also sturdy—too much to list here. In many ways explaining what goes into an airplane is like explaining to someone that there's pipes under the sink below that beautiful faucet.

---

3 Nachiappan Nagappan et al., "Realizing Quality Improvement through Test Driven Development: Results and Experience of Four Industrial Teams," *Empirical Software Engineering* 13, no. 3 (2008): 289–302, *http://bit.ly/Nagappanetal*.

Refactoring takes the existing structure and makes it better. It's taking a messy circuit breaker and cleaning it up so that when you look at it, you know exactly what is going on. While airplanes are rigidly designed, software is not. Things change rapidly in software. Many companies are continuously deploying software to a production environment. All of that feature development can sometimes cause a certain amount of technical debt.

Technical debt, also known as *design debt* or *code debt*, is a metaphor for poor system design that happens over time with software projects. The debilitating problem of technical debt is that it accrues interest and eventually blocks future feature development.

If you've been on a project long enough, you will know the feeling of having fast releases in the beginning only to come to a standstill toward the end. Technical debt in many cases arises through not writing tests or not following the SOLID principles.

Having technical debt isn't a bad thing—sometimes projects need to be pushed out earlier so business can expand—but not paying down debt will eventually accrue enough interest to destroy a project. The way we get over this is by refactoring our code.

By refactoring, we move our code closer to the SOLID guidelines and a TDD codebase. It's cleaning up the existing code and making it easy for new developers to come in and work on the code that exists like so:

1. Follow the SOLID guidelines
   a. Single Responsibility Principle
   b. Open/Closed Principle
   c. Liskov Substitution Principle
   d. Interface Segregation Principle
   e. Dependency Inversion Principle
2. Implement TDD (test-driven development/design)
3. Refactor your code to avoid a buildup of technical debt

The real question now is what makes the software right?

Writing the Right Software

Writing the right software is much trickier than writing software right. In his book *Specification by Example*, Gojko Adzic determines the best approach to writing software is to craft specifications first, then to work with consumers directly. Only after the specification is complete does one write the code to fit that spec. But this suffers from the problem of practice—sometimes the world isn't what we think it is. Our initial model of what we think is true many times isn't.

Webvan, for instance, failed miserably at building an online grocery business. They had almost $400 million in investment capital and rapidly built infrastructure to support what they thought would be a booming business. Unfortunately they were a flop because of the cost of shipping food and the overestimated market for online grocery buying. By many measures they were a success at writing software and building a business, but the market just wasn't ready for them and they quickly went bankrupt. Today a lot of the infrastructure they built is used by Amazon.com for AmazonFresh.

> In theory, theory and practice are the same. In practice they are not.
>
> —Albert Einstein

We are now at the point where theoretically we can write software correctly and it'll work, but writing the right software is a much fuzzier problem. This is where machine learning really comes in.

Writing the Right Software with Machine Learning

In *The Knowledge-Creating Company*, Nonaka and Takeuchi outlined what made Japanese companies so successful in the 1980s. Instead of a top-down approach of solving the problem, they would learn over time. Their example of kneading bread and turning that into a breadmaker is a perfect example of iteration and is easily applied to software development.

But we can go further with machine learning.

What Exactly Is Machine Learning?

According to most definitions, machine learning is a collection of algorithms, techniques, and tricks of the trade that allow machines to learn from data—that is, something represented in numerical format (matrices, vectors, etc.).

To understand machine learning better, though, let's look at how it came into existence. In the 1950s extensive research was done on playing checkers. A lot of these models focused on playing the game better and coming up with optimal strategies. You could probably come up with a simple enough program to play checkers today just by working backward from a win, mapping out a decision tree, and optimizing that way.

Yet this was a very narrow and deductive way of reasoning. Effectively the agent had to be programmed. In most of these early programs there was no context or irrational behavior programmed in.

About 30 years later, machine learning started to take off. Many of the same minds started working on problems involving spam filtering, classification, and general data analysis.

The important shift here is a move away from computerized deduction to computerized induction. Much as Sherlock Holmes did, deduction involves using complex logic models to come to a conclusion. By contrast, induction involves taking data as being true and trying to fit a model to that data. This shift has created many great advances in finding good-enough solutions to common problems.

The issue with inductive reasoning, though, is that you can only feed the algorithm data that *you* know about. Quantifying some things is exceptionally difficult. For instance, how could you quantify how cuddly a kitten looks in an image?

In the last 10 years we have been witnessing a renaissance around deep learning, which alleviates that problem. Instead of relying on data coded by humans, algorithms like autoencoders have been able to find data points we couldn't quantify before.

This all sounds amazing, but with all this power comes an exceptionally high cost and responsibility.

The High Interest Credit Card Debt of Machine Learning

Recently, in a paper published by Google titled "Machine Learning: The High Interest Credit Card of Technical Debt" (*http://research.google.com/pubs/pub43146.html*), Sculley et al. explained that machine learning projects suffer from the same technical debt issues outlined plus more (Table 1-1).

They noted that machine learning projects are inherently complex, have vague boundaries, rely heavily on data dependencies, suffer from system-level spaghetti code, and can radically change due to changes in the outside world. Their argument is that these are specifically related to machine learning projects and for the most part they are.

Instead of going through these issues one by one, I thought it would be more interesting to tie back to our original discussion of SOLID and TDD as well as refactoring and see how it relates to machine learning code.

Table 1-1. The high interest credit card debt of machine learning

Machine learning problem	Manifests as	SOLID violation
Entanglement	Changing one factor changes everything	SRP
Hidden feedback loops	Having built-in hidden features in model	OCP
Undeclared consumers/visibility debt		ISP
Unstable data dependencies	Volatile data	ISP

Machine learning problem	Manifests as	SOLID violation
Underutilized data dependencies	Unused dimensions	LSP
Correction cascade		*
Glue code	Writing code that does everything	SRP
Pipeline jungles	Sending data through complex workflow	DIP
Experimental paths	Dead paths that go nowhere	DIP
Configuration debt	Using old configurations for new data	*
Fixed thresholds in a dynamic world	Not being flexible to changes in correlations	*
Correlations change	Modeling correlation over causation	ML Specific

SOLID Applied to Machine Learning

SOLID, as you remember, is just a guideline reminding us to follow certain goals when writing object-oriented code. Many machine learning algorithms are inherently not object oriented. They are functional, mathematical, and use lots of statistics, but that doesn't have to be the case. Instead of thinking of things in purely functional terms, we can strive to use objects around each row vector and matrix of data.

SRP

In machine learning code, one of the biggest challenges for people to realize is that the code and the data are dependent on each other. Without the data the machine learning algorithm is worthless, and without the machine learning algorithm we wouldn't know what to do with the data. So by definition they are tightly intertwined and coupled. This tightly coupled dependency is probably one of the biggest reasons that machine learning projects fail.

This dependency manifests as two problems in machine learning code: entanglement and glue code. *Entanglement* is sometimes called the principle of Changing Anything Changes Everything or CACE. The simplest example is probabilities. If you remove one probability from a distribution, then all the rest have to adjust. This is a violation of SRP.

Possible mitigation strategies include isolating models, analyzing dimensional dependencies,[4] and regularization techniques.[5] We will return to this problem when we review Bayesian models and probability models.

---

4 H. B. McMahan et al., "Ad Click Prediction: A View from the Trenches." In *The 19th ACM SIGKDD International Conference on Knowledge Discovery and Data Mining, KDD 2013*, Chicago, IL, August 11–14, 2013.

5 A. Lavoie et al., "History Dependent Domain Adaptation." In *Domain Adaptation Workshop at NIPS '11*, 2011.

Glue code is the code that accumulates over time in a coding project. Its purpose is usually to glue two separate pieces together inelegantly. It also tends to be the type of code that tries to solve all problems instead of just one.

Whether machine learning researchers want to admit it or not, many times the actual machine learning algorithms themselves are quite simple. The surrounding code is what makes up the bulk of the project. Depending on what library you use, whether it be GraphLab, MATLAB, scikit-learn, or R, they all have their own implementation of vectors and matrices, which is what machine learning mostly comes down to.

OCP

Recall that the OCP is about opening classes for extension but not modification. One way this manifests in machine learning code is the problem of CACE. This can manifest in any software project but in machine learning projects it is often seen as hidden feedback loops.

A good example of a hidden feedback loop is *predictive policing*. Over the last few years, many researchers have shown that machine learning algorithms can be applied to determine where crimes will occur. Preliminary results have shown that these algorithms work exceptionally well. But unfortunately there is a dark side to them as well.

While these algorithms can show where crimes will happen, what will naturally occur is the police will start patrolling those areas more and finding more crimes there, and as a result will self-reinforce the algorithm. This could also be called confirmation bias, or the bias of confirming our preconceived notion, and also has the downside of enforcing systematic discrimination against certain demographics or neighborhoods.

While hidden feedback loops are hard to detect, they should be watched for with a keen eye and taken out.

LSP

Not a lot of people talk about the LSP anymore because many programmers are advocating for composition over inheritance these days. But in the machine learning world, the LSP is violated a lot. Many times we are given data sets that we don't have all the answers for yet. Sometimes these data sets are thousands of dimensions wide.

Running algorithms against those data sets can actually violate the LSP. One common manifestation in machine learning code is underutilized data dependencies. Many times we are given data sets that include thousands of dimensions, which can sometimes yield pertinent information and sometimes not. Our models might take all dimensions yet use one infrequently. So for instance, in classifying mushrooms as either poisonous or edible, information like odor can be a big indicator while ring number isn't. The ring number has low granularity and can only be zero, one, or two; thus it really doesn't add much to our model of classifying mushrooms. So that information could be trimmed out of our model and wouldn't greatly degrade performance.

You might be thinking why this is related to the LSP, and the reason is if we can use only the smallest set of datapoints (or features), we have built the best model possible. This also aligns well with Ockham's Razor, which states that the simplest solution is the best one.

ISP

The ISP is the notion that a client-specific interface is better than a general purpose one. In machine learning projects this can often be hard to enforce because of the tight coupling of data to the code. In machine learning code, the ISP is usually violated by two types of problems: *visibility debt* and *unstable data*.

Take for instance the case where a company has a reporting database that is used to collect information about sales, shipping data, and other pieces of crucial information. This is all managed through some sort of project that gets the data into this database. The customer that this database defines is a machine learning project that takes previous sales data to predict the sales for the future. Then one day during cleanup, someone renames a table that used to be called something very confusing to something much more useful. All hell breaks loose and people are wondering what happened.

What ended up happening is that the machine learning project wasn't the only consumer of the data; six Access databases were attached to it, too. The fact that there were that many undeclared consumers is in itself a piece of debt for a machine learning project.

This type of debt is called visibility debt and while it mostly doesn't affect a project's stability, sometimes, as features are built, at some point it will hold everything back.

Data is dependent on the code used to make inductions from it, so building a stable project requires having stable data. Many times this just isn't the case. Take for instance the price of a stock; in the morning it might be valuable but hours later become worthless.

This ends up violating the ISP because we are looking at the general data stream instead of one specific to the client, which can make portfolio trading algorithms very difficult to build. One common trick is to build some sort of exponential weighting scheme around data; another more important one is to version data streams. This versioned scheme serves as a viable way to limit the volatility of a model's predictions.

DIP

The Dependency Inversion Principle is about limiting our buildups of data and making code more flexible for future changes. In a machine learning project we see concretions happen in two specific ways: *pipeline jungles* and *experimental paths*.

Pipeline jungles are common in data-driven projects and are almost a form of glue code. This is the amalgamation of data being prepared and moved around. In some cases this code is tying everything together so the model can work with the prepared data. Unfortunately, though, over time these jungles start to grow complicated and unusable.

Machine learning code requires both software and data. They are intertwined and inseparable. Sometimes, then, we have to test things during production. Sometimes tests on our machines give us false hope and we need to experiment with a line of code. Those experimental paths add up over time and end up polluting our workspace. The best way of reducing the associated debt is to introduce tombstoning, which is an old technique from C.

Tombstones are a method of marking something as ready to be deleted. If the method is called in production it will log an event to a logfile that can be used to sweep the codebase later.

For those of you who have studied garbage collection you most likely have heard of this method as mark and sweep. Basically you mark an object as ready to be deleted and later sweep marked objects out.

Machine Learning Code Is Complex but Not Impossible

At times, machine learning code can be difficult to write and understand, but it is far from impossible. Remember the flight analogy we began with, and use the SOLID guidelines as your "preflight" checklist for writing successful machine learning code —while complex, it doesn't have to be complicated.

In the same vein, you can compare machine learning code to flying a spaceship—it's certainly been done before, but it's still bleeding edge. With the SOLID checklist model, we can launch our code effectively using TDD and refactoring. In essence, writing successful machine learning code comes down to being disciplined enough to follow the principles of design we've laid out in this chapter, and writing tests to support your code-based hypotheses. Another critical element in writing effective code is being flexible and adapting to the changes it will encounter in the real world.

TDD: Scientific Method 2.0

Every true scientist is a dreamer and a skeptic. Daring to put a person on the moon was audacious, but through systematic research and development we have accomplished that and much more. The same is true with machine learning code. Some of the applications are fascinating but also hard to pull off.

The secret to doing so is to use the checklist of SOLID for machine learning and the tools of TDD and refactoring to get us there.

TDD is more of a style of problem solving, not a mandate from above. What testing gives us is a feedback loop that we can use to work through tough problems. As scientists would assert that they need to first hypothesize, test, and theorize, we can assert that as a TDD practitioner, the process of red (the tests fail), green (the tests pass), refactor is just as viable.

This book will delve heavily into applying not only TDD but also SOLID principles to machine learning, with the goal being to refactor our way to building a stable, scalable, and easy-to-use model.

Refactoring Our Way to Knowledge

As mentioned, refactoring is the ability to edit one's work and to rethink what was once stated. Throughout the book we will talk about refactoring common machine learning pitfalls as it applies to algorithms.

The Plan for the Book

This book will cover a lot of ground with machine learning, but by the end you should have a better grasp of how to write machine learning code as well as how to deploy to a production environment and operate at scale. Machine learning is a fascinating field that can achieve much, but without discipline, checklists, and guidelines, many machine learning projects are doomed to fail.

Throughout the book we will tie back to the original principles in this chapter by talking about SOLID principles, testing our code (using various means), and refactoring as a way to continually learn from and improve the performance of our code.

Every chapter will explain the Python packages we will use and describe a general testing plan. While machine learning code isn't testable in a one-to-one case, it ends up being something for which we can write tests to help our knowledge of the problem.

## CHAPTER 2

A Quick Introduction to Machine Learning

You've picked up this book because you're interested in machine learning. While you probably have an idea of what machine learning is, the subject is often defined somewhat vaguely. In this quick introduction, I'll go over what exactly machine learning is, and provide a general framework for thinking about machine learning algorithms.

What Is Machine Learning?

Machine learning is the intersection between theoretically sound computer science and practically noisy data. Essentially, it's about machines making sense out of data in much the same way that humans do.

Machine learning is a type of artificial intelligence whereby an algorithm or method extracts patterns from data. Machine learning solves a few general problems; these are listed in Table 2-1 and described in the subsections that follow.

Table 2-1. The problems that machine learning can solve

Problem	Machine learning category
Fitting some data to a function or function approximation	Supervised learning
Figuring out what the data is without any feedback	Unsupervised learning
Maximizing rewards over time	Reinforcement learning

Supervised Learning

Supervised learning, or function approximation, is simply fitting data to a function of any variety. For instance, given the noisy data shown in Figure 2-1, you can fit a line that generally approximates it.

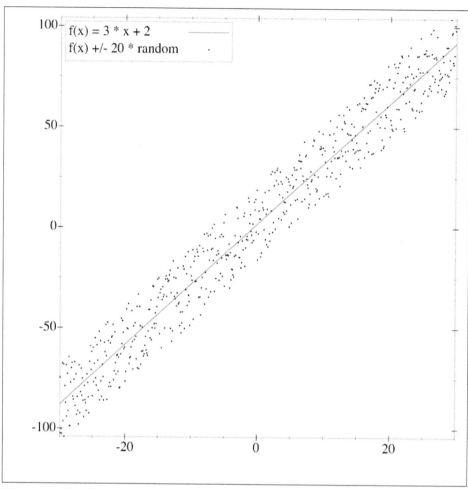

Figure 2-1. This data fits quite well to a straight line

Unsupervised Learning

Unsupervised learning involves figuring out what makes the data special. For instance, if we were given many data points, we could group them by similarity (Figure 2-2), or perhaps determine which variables are better than others.

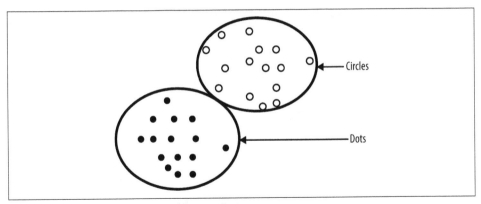

Figure 2-2. Two clusters grouped by similarity

Reinforcement Learning

Reinforcement learning involves figuring out how to play a multistage game with rewards and payoffs. Think of it as the algorithms that optimize the life of something. A common example of a reinforcement learning algorithm is a mouse trying to find cheese in a maze. For the most part, the mouse gets zero reward until it finally finds the cheese.

We will discuss supervised and unsupervised learning in this book but skip reinforcement learning. In the final chapter, I include some resources that you can check out if you'd like to learn more about reinforcement learning.

What Can Machine Learning Accomplish?

What makes machine learning unique is its ability to optimally figure things out. But each machine learning algorithm has quirks and trade-offs. Some do better than others. This book covers quite a few algorithms, so Table 2-2 provides a matrix to help you navigate them and determine how useful each will be to you.

Table 2-2. Machine learning algorithm matrix

Algorithm	Learning type	Class	Restriction bias	Preference bias
K-Nearest Neighbors	Supervised	Instance based	Generally speaking, KNN is good for measuring distance-based approximations; it suffers from the curse of dimensionality	Prefers problems that are distance based
Naive Bayes	Supervised	Probabilistic	Works on problems where the inputs are independent from each other	Prefers problems where the probability will always be greater than zero for each class

Algorithm	Learning type	Class	Restriction bias	Preference bias
Decision Trees/ Random Forests	Supervised	Tree	Becomes less useful on problems with low covariance	Prefers problems with categorical data
Support Vector Machines	Supervised	Decision boundary	Works where there is a definite distinction between two classifications	Prefers binary classification problems
Neural Networks	Supervised	Nonlinear functional approximation	Little restriction bias	Prefers binary inputs
Hidden Markov Models	Supervised/ Unsupervised	Markovian	Generally works well for system information where the Markov assumption holds	Prefers time-series data and memoryless information
Clustering	Unsupervised	Clustering	No restriction	Prefers data that is in groupings given some form of distance (Euclidean, Manhattan, or others)
Feature Selection	Unsupervised	Matrix factorization	No restrictions	Depending on algorithm can prefer data with high mutual information
Feature Transformation	Unsupervised	Matrix factorization	Must be a nondegenerate matrix	Will work much better on matricies that don't have inversion issues
Bagging	Meta-heuristic	Meta-heuristic	Will work on just about anything	Prefers data that isn't highly variable

Refer to this matrix throughout the book to understand how these algorithms relate to one another.

Machine learning is only as good as what it applies to, so let's get to implementing some of these algorithms! Before we get started, you will need to install Python, which you can do at *https://www.python.org/downloads/*. This book was tested using Python 3.5, but most likely it will work with Python 2.7.x as well. All of those changes will be annotated in the book's coding resources, which are available on GitHub (*https://github.com/thoughtfulml/examples-in-python*).

Mathematical Notation Used Throughout the Book

This book uses mathematics to solve problems, but all of the examples are programmer-centric. Throughout the book, I'll use the mathematical notations shown in Table 2-3.

Table 2-3. Mathematical notations used in this book's examples

Symbol	How do you say it?	What does it do?
$\sum_{i=0}^{n} x_i$	The sum of all xs from x_0 to x_n	This is the same thing as $x_0 + x_1 + \cdots + x_n$.
$|x|$	The absolute value of x	This takes any value of x and makes it positive. So $|-x| = |x|$.
$\sqrt{4}$	The square root of 4	This is the opposite of 2^2.
$z_k = <0.5, 0.5>$	Vector z_k equals 0.5 and 0.5	This is a point on the xy plane and is denoted as a vector, which is a group of numerical points.
$log_2(2)$	Log 2	This solves for i in $2^i = 2$.
$P(A)$	Probability of A	In many cases, this is the count of A divided by the total occurrences.
$P(A|B)$	Probability of A given B	This is the probability of A and B divided by the probability of B.
$\{1,2,3\} \cap \{1\}$	The intersection of set one and two	This turns into a set $\{1\}$.
$\{1,2,3\} \cup \{4,1\}$	The union of set one and two	This equates to $\{1,2,3,4\}$.
$det(C)$	The determinant of the matrix C	This will help determine whether a matrix is invertible or not.
$a \propto b$	a is proportional to b	This means that $m \cdot a = b$.
$min\ f(x)$	Minimize $f(x)$	This is an objective function to minimize the function $f(x)$.
X^T	Transpose of the matrix X	Take all elements of the matrix and switch the row with the column.

Conclusion

This isn't an exhaustive introduction to machine learning, but that's okay. There's always going to be a lot for us all to learn when it comes to this complex subject, but for the remainder of this book, this should serve us well in approaching these problems.

## CHAPTER 3

K-Nearest Neighbors

Have you ever bought a house before? If you're like a lot of people around the world, the joy of owning your own home is exciting, but the process of finding and buying a house can be stressful. Whether we're in a economic boom or recession, everybody wants to get the best house for the most reasonable price.

But how would you go about buying a house? How do you appraise a house? How does a company like Zillow come up with their Zestimates? We'll spend most of this chapter answering questions related to this fundamental concept: distance-based approximations.

First we'll talk about how we can estimate a house's value. Then we'll discuss how to classify houses into categories such as "Buy," "Hold," and "Sell." At that point we'll talk about a general algorithm, K-Nearest Neighbors, and how it can be used to solve problems such as this. We'll break it down into a few sections of what makes something near, as well as what a neighborhood really is (i.e., what is the optimal K for something?).

How Do You Determine Whether You Want to Buy a House?

This question has plagued many of us for a long time. If you are going out to buy a house, or calculating whether it's better to rent, you are most likely trying to answer this question implicitly. Home appraisals are a tricky subject, and are notorious for drift with calculations. For instance on Zillow's website they explain that their famous Zestimate is flawed (*http://bit.ly/Zestimate-whatis*). They state that based on where you are looking, the value might drift by a localized amount.

Location is really key with houses. Seattle might have a different demand curve than San Francisco, which makes complete sense if you know housing! The question of whether to buy or not comes down to value amortized over the course of how long you're living there. But how do you come up with a value?

How Valuable Is That House?

Things are worth as much as someone is willing to pay.

—Old Saying

 Valuing a house is tough business. Even if we were able to come up with a model with many endogenous variables that make a huge difference, it doesn't cover up the fact that buying a house is subjective and sometimes includes a bidding war. These are almost impossible to predict. You're more than welcome to use this to value houses, but there will be errors that take years of experience to overcome.

A house is worth as much as it'll sell for. The answer to how valuable a house is, at its core, is simple but difficult to estimate. Due to inelastic supply, or because houses are all fairly unique, home sale prices have a tendency to be erratic. Sometimes you just love a house and will pay a premium for it.

But let's just say that the house is worth what someone will pay for it. This is a function based on a bag of attributes associated with houses. We might determine that a good approach to estimating house values would be:

Equation 3-1. House value

$$HouseValue = f(Space, LandSize, Rooms, Bathrooms, \cdots)$$

This model could be found through regression (which we'll cover in Chapter 5) or other approximation algorithms, but this is missing a major component of real estate: "Location, Location, Location!" To overcome this, we can come up with something called a hedonic regression.

Hedonic Regression

 You probably already know of a frequently used real-life hedonic regression: the CPI index (*http://www.bls.gov/cpi/*). This is used as a way of decomposing baskets of items that people commonly buy to come up with an index for inflation.

Economics is a dismal science because we're trying to approximate rational behaviors. Unfortunately we are predictably irrational (shout-out to Dan Ariely). But a good algorithm for valuing houses that is similar to what home appraisers use is called hedonic regression.

The general idea with hard-to-value items like houses that don't have a highly liquid market and suffer from subjectivity is that there are externalities that we can't directly estimate. For instance, how would you estimate pollution, noise, or neighbors who are jerks?

To overcome this, hedonic regression takes a different approach than general regression. Instead of focusing on fitting a curve to a bag of attributes, it focuses on the components of a house. For instance, the hedonic method allows you to find out how much a bedroom costs (on average).

Take a look at the Table 3-1, which compares housing prices with number of bedrooms. From here we can fit a naive approximation of value to bedroom number, to come up with an estimate of cost per bedroom.

Table 3-1. House price by number of bedrooms

Price (in $1,000)	Bedrooms
$899	4
$399	3
$749	3
$649	3

This is extremely useful for valuing houses because as consumers, we can use this to focus on what matters to us and decompose houses into whether they're overpriced because of bedroom numbers or the fact that they're right next to a park.

This gets us to the next improvement, which is location. Even with hedonic regression, we suffer from the problem of location. A bedroom in SoHo in London, England is probably more expensive than a bedroom in Mumbai, India. So for that we need to focus on the neighborhood.

What Is a Neighborhood?

The value of a house is often determined by its neighborhood. For instance, in Seattle, an apartment in Capitol Hill is more expensive than one in Lake City. Generally speaking, the cost of commuting is worth half of your hourly wage plus maintenance and gas,[1] so a neighborhood closer to the economic center is more valuable.

But how would we focus only on the neighborhood?

Theoretically we could come up with an elegant solution using something like an exponential decay function that weights houses closer to downtown higher and farther houses lower. Or we could come up with something static that works exceptionally well: K-Nearest Neighbors.

K-Nearest Neighbors

What if we were to come up with a solution that is inelegant but works just as well? Say we were to assert that we will only look at an arbitrary amount of houses near to a similar house we're looking at. Would that also work?

Surprisingly, yes. This is the K-Nearest Neighbor (KNN) solution, which performs exceptionally well. It takes two forms: a regression, where we want a value, or a classification. To apply KNN to our problem of house values, we would just have to find the nearest K neighbors.

The KNN algorithm was originally introduced by Drs. Evelyn Fix and J. L. Hodges Jr, in an unpublished technical report written for the U.S. Air Force School of Aviation Medicine. Fix and Hodges' original research focused on splitting up classification problems into a few subproblems:

- Distributions F and G are completely known.
- Distributions F and G are completely known except for a few parameters.
- F and G are unknown, except possibly for the existence of densities.

Fix and Hodges pointed out that if you know the distributions of two classifications or you know the distribution minus some parameters, you can easily back out useful solutions. Therefore, they focused their work on the more difficult case of finding classifications among distributions that are unknown. What they came up with laid the groundwork for the KNN algorithm.

This opens a few more questions:

- What are neighbors, and what makes them near?
- How do we pick the arbitrary number of neighbors, K?

---

1 Van Ommeren et al., "Estimating the Marginal Willingness to Pay for Commuting," *Journal of Regional Science* 40 (2000): 541–63.

- What do we do with the neighbors afterward?

Mr. K's Nearest Neighborhood

We all implicitly know what a neighborhood is. Whether you live in the woods or a row of brownstones, we all live in a neighborhood of sorts. A neighborhood for lack of a better definition could just be called a cluster of houses (we'll get to clustering later).

A cluster at this point could be just thought of as a tight grouping of houses or items in *n* dimensions. But what denotes a "tight grouping"? Since you've most likely taken a geometry class at some time in your life, you're probably thinking of the Pythagorean theorem or something similar, but things aren't quite that simple. Distances are a class of functions that can be much more complex.

Distances

> As the crow flies.
>
> —Old Saying

Geometry class taught us that if you sum the square of two sides of a triangle and take its square root, you'll have the side of the hypotenuse or the third side (Figure 3-1). This as we all know is the Pythagorean theorem, but distances can be much more complicated. Distances can take many different forms but generally there are geometrical, computational, and statistical distances which we'll discuss in this section.

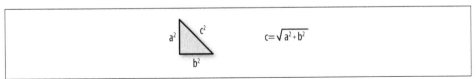

Figure 3-1. Pythagorean theorem

Triangle Inequality

One interesting aspect about the triangle in Figure 3-1 is that the length of the hypotenuse is always less than the length of each side added up individually (Figure 3-2).

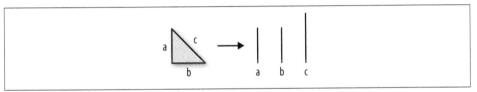

Figure 3-2. Triangle broken into three line segments

Stated mathematically: $\|x + y\| \le \|x\| + \|y\|$. This inequality is important for finding a distance function; if the triangle inequality didn't hold, what would happen is distances would become slightly distorted as you measure distance between points in a Euclidean space.

Geometrical Distance

The most intuitive distance functions are geometrical. Intuitively we can measure how far something is from one point to another. We already know about the Pythagorean theorem, but there are an infinite amount of possibilities that satisfy the triangle inequality.

Stated mathematically we can take the Pythagorean theorem and build what is called the Euclidean distance, which is denoted as:

$$d(x, y) = \sqrt{\Sigma_{i=0}^{n}(x_i - y_i)^2}$$

As you can see, this is similar to the Pythagorean theorem, except it includes a sum. Mathematics gives us even greater ability to build distances by using something called a Minkowski distance (see Figure 3-3):

$$d_p(x, y) = \left(\Sigma_{i=0}^{n}|x_i - y_i|^p\right)^{\frac{1}{p}}$$

This p can be any integer and still satisfy the triangle inequality.

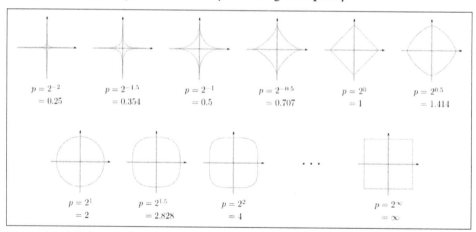

Figure 3-3. Minkowski distances as n increases (Source: Wikimedia)

Cosine similarity

One last geometrical distance is called cosine similarity or cosine distance. The beauty of this distance is its sheer speed at calculating distances between sparse vectors. For instance if we had 1,000 attributes collected about houses and 300 of these were mutually exclusive (meaning that one house had them but the others don't), then we would only need to include 700 dimensions in the calculation.

Visually this measures the inner product space between two vectors and presents us with cosine as a measure. Its function is:

$$d(x, y) = \frac{x \cdot y}{\| x \| \, \| y \|}$$

where $\|x\|$ denotes the Euclidean distance discussed earlier.

Geometrical distances are generally what we want. When we talk about houses we want a geometrical distance. But there are other spaces that are just as valuable: computational, or discrete, as well as statistical distances.

Computational Distances

Imagine you want to measure how far it is from one part of the city to another. One way of doing this would be to utilize coordinates (longitude, latitude) and calculate a Euclidean distance. Let's say you're at Saint Edward State Park in Kenmore, WA (47.7329290, -122.2571466) and you want to meet someone at Vivace Espresso on Capitol Hill, Seattle, WA (47.6216650, -122.3213002).

Using the Euclidean distance we would calculate:

$$\sqrt{(47.73 - 47.62)^2 + (-122.26 + 122.32)^2} \approx 0.13$$

This is obviously a small result as it's in degrees of latitude and longitude. To convert this into miles we would multiply it by 69.055, which yields approximately 8.9 miles (14.32 kilometers). Unfortunately this is way off! The actual distance is 14.2 miles (22.9 kilometers). Why are things so far off?

 Note that 69.055 is actually an approximation of latitude degrees to miles. Earth is an ellipsoid and therefore calculating distances actually depends on where you are in the world. But for such a short distance it's good enough.

If I had the ability to lift off from Saint Edward State Park and fly to Vivace then, yes, it'd be shorter, but if I were to walk or drive I'd have to drive around Lake Washington (see Figure 3-4).

This gets us to the motivation behind computational distances. If you were to drive from Saint Edward State Park to Vivace then you'd have to follow the constraints of a road.

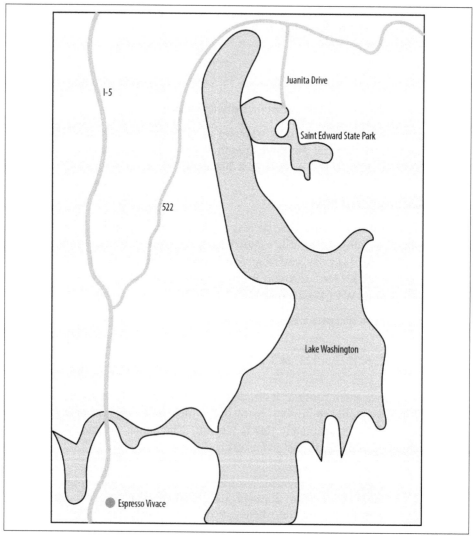

Figure 3-4. Driving to Vivace from Saint Edward State Park

Manhattan distance

This gets us into what is called the Taxicab distance or Manhattan distance.

Equation 3-2. Manhattan distance

$$\sum_{i=0}^{n} |x_i - y_i|$$

Note that there is no ability to travel out of bounds. So imagine that your metric space is a grid of graphing paper and you are only allowed to draw along the boxes.

The Manhattan distance can be used for problems such as traversal of a graph and discrete optimization problems where you are constrained by edges. With our housing example, most likely you would want to measure the value of houses that are close by driving, not by flying. Otherwise you might include houses in your search that are across a barrier like a lake, or a mountain!

Levenshtein distance

Another distance that is commonly used in natural language processing is the Levenshtein distance. An analogy of how Levenshtein distance works is by changing one neighborhood to make an exact copy of another. The number of steps to make that happen is the distance. Usually this is applied with strings of characters to determine how many deletions, additions, or substitutions the strings require to be equal.

This can be quite useful for determining how similar neighborhoods are as well as strings. The formula for this is a bit more complicated as it is a recursive function, so instead of looking at the math we'll just write Python for this:

```python
def lev(a, b):
    if not a: return len(b)
    if not b: return len(a)
    return min(lev(a[1:], b[1:])+(a[0] != b[0]), lev(a[1:], b)+1, lev(a, b[1:])+1)
```

 This is an extremely slow algorithm and I'm only putting it here for understanding, not to actually implement. If you'd like to implement Levenshtein, you will need to use dynamic programming to have good performance.

Statistical Distances

Last, there's a third class of distances that I call statistical distances. In statistics we're taught that to measure volatility or variance, we take pairs of datapoints and measure the squared difference. This gives us an idea of how dispersed the population is. This can actually be used when calculating distance as well, using what is called the Mahalanobis distance.

Imagine for a minute that you want to measure distance in an affluent neighborhood that is right on the water. People love living on the water and the closer you are to it, the higher the home value. But with our distances discussed earlier, whether computational or geometrical, we would have a bad approximation of this particular neighborhood because those distance calculations are primarily spherical in nature (Figures 3-5 and 3-6).

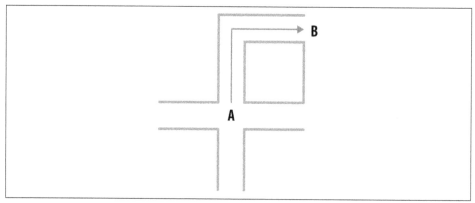

Figure 3-5. Driving from point A to point B on a city block

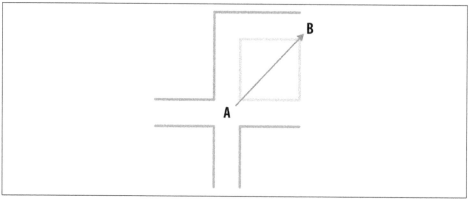

Figure 3-6. Straight line between A and B

This seems like a bad approach for this neighborhood because it is not spherical in nature. If we were to use Euclidean distances we'd be measuring values of houses not on the beach. If we were to use Manhattan distances we'd only look at houses close by the road.

Mahalanobis distance

Another approach is using the Mahalanobis distance. This takes into consideration some other statistical factors:

$$d(x, y) = \sqrt{\Sigma_{i=1}^{n} \frac{(x_i - y_i)^2}{s_i^2}}$$

What this effectively does is give more stretch to the grouping of items (Figure 3-7):

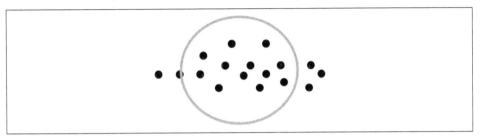

Figure 3-7. Mahalanobis distance

Jaccard distance

Yet another distance metric is called the Jaccard distance. This takes into consideration the population of overlap. For instance, if the number of attributes for one house match another, then they would be overlapping and therefore close in distance, whereas if the houses had diverging attributes they wouldn't match. This is primarily used to quickly determine how similar text is by counting up the frequencies of letters in a string and then counting the characters that are not the same across both. Its formula is:

$$J(X, Y) = \frac{|X \cap Y|}{|X \cup Y|}$$

This finishes up a primer on distances. Now that we know how to measure what is close and what is far, how do we go about building a grouping or neighborhood? How many houses should be in the neighborhood?

Curse of Dimensionality

Before we continue, there's a serious concern with using distances for anything and that is called the *curse of dimensionality*. When we model high-dimension spaces, our approximations of distance become less reliable. In practice it is important to realize that finding features of data sets is essential to making a resilient model. We will talk about feature engineering in Chapter 10 but for now be cognizant of the problem. Figure 3-8 shows a visual way of thinking about this.

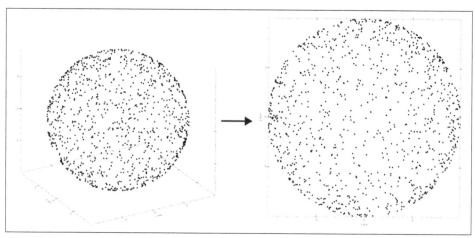

Figure 3-8. Curse of dimensionality

As Figure 3-8 shows, when we put random dots on a unit sphere and measure the distance from the origin (0,0,0), we find that the distance is always 1. But if we were to project that onto a 2D space, the distance would be less than or equal to 1. This same truth holds when we expand the dimensions. For instance, if we expanded our set from 3 dimensions to 4, it would be greater than or equal to 1. This inability to center in on a consistent distance is what breaks distance-based models, because all of the data points become chaotic and move away from one another.

How Do We Pick K?

Picking the number of houses to put into this model is a difficult problem—easy to verify but hard to calculate beforehand. At this point we know how we want to group things, but just don't know how many items to put into our neighborhood. There are a few approaches to determining an optimal K, each with their own set of downsides:

- Guessing
- Using a heuristic
- Optimizing using an algorithm

Guessing K

Guessing is always a good solution. Many times when we are approaching a problem, we have domain knowledge of it. Whether we are an expert or not, we know about the problem enough to know what a neighborhood is. My neighborhood where I live, for instance, is roughly 12 houses. If I wanted to expand I could set my K to 30 for a more flattened-out approximation.

Heuristics for Picking K

There are three heuristics that can help you determine an optimal K for a KNN algorithm:

1. Use coprime class and K combinations
2. Choose a K that is greater or equal to the number of classes plus one
3. Choose a K that is low enough to avoid noise

Use coprime class and K combinations

Picking coprime numbers of classes and K will ensure fewer ties. Coprime numbers are two numbers that don't share any common divisors except for 1. So, for instance, 4 and 9 are coprime while 3 and 9 are not. Imagine you have two classes, good and bad. If we were to pick a K of 6, which is even, then we might end up having ties. Graphically it looks like Figure 3-9.

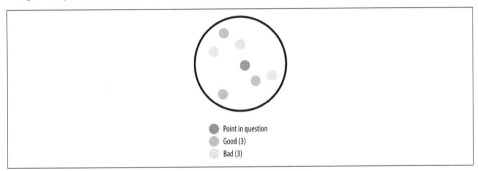

Figure 3-9. Tie with K=6 and two classes

If you picked a K of 5 instead (Figure 3-10), there wouldn't be a tie.

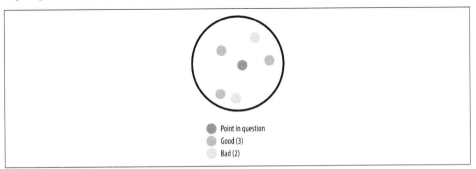

Figure 3-10. K=5 with two classes and no tie

Choose a K that is greater or equal to the number of classes plus one

Imagine there are three classes: lawful, chaotic, and neutral. A good heuristic is to pick a K of at least 3 because anything less will mean that there is no chance that each class will be represented. To illustrate, Figure 3-11 shows the case of K=2.

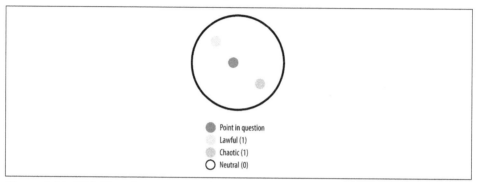

Figure 3-11. With K=2 there is no possibility that all three classes will be represented

Note how there are only two classes that get the chance to be used. Again, this is why we need to use at least K=3. But based on what we found in the first heuristic, ties are not a good thing. So, really, instead of K=3, we should use K=4 (as shown in Figure 3-12).

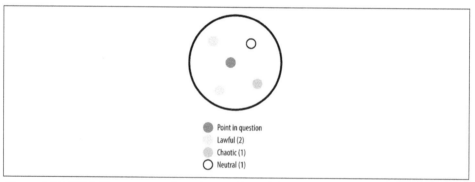

Figure 3-12. With K set greater than the number of classes, there is a chance for all classes to be represented

Choose a K that is low enough to avoid noise

As K increases, you eventually approach the size of the entire data set. If you were to pick the entire data set, you would select the most common class. A simple example is mapping a customer's affinity to a brand. Say you have 100 orders as shown in Table 3-2.

Table 3-2. Brand to count

Brand	Count
Widget Inc.	30
Bozo Group	23
Robots and Rockets	12
Ion 5	35
Total	100

If we were to set K=100, our answer will always be Ion 5 because Ion 5 is the distribution (the most common class) of the order history. That is not really what we want; instead, we want to determine the most recent order affinity. More specifically, we want to minimize the amount of noise that comes into our classification. Without coming up with a specific algorithm for this, we can justify K being set to a much lower rate, like K=3 or K=11.

Algorithms for picking K

Picking K can be somewhat qualitative and nonscientific, and that's why there are many algorithms showing how to optimize K over a given training set. There are many approaches to choosing K, ranging from genetic algorithms to brute force to grid searches. Many people assert that you should determine K based on domain knowledge that you have as the implementor. For instance, if you know that 5 is good enough, you can pick that. This problem where you are trying to minimize error based on an arbitrary K is known as a *hill climbing problem*. The idea is to iterate through a couple of possible Ks until you find a suitable error. The difficult part about finding a K using an approach like genetic algorithms or brute force is that as K increases, the complexity of the classification also increases and slows down performance. In other words, as you increase K, the program actually gets slower. If you want to learn more about genetic algorithms applied to finding an optimal K, you can read more about it in Nigsch et al.'s *Journal of Chemical Information and Modeling* article, "Melting Point Prediction Employing k-Nearest Neighbor Algorithms and Genetic Parameter Optimization." Personally, I think iterating twice through 1% of the population size is good enough. You should have a decent idea of what works and what doesn't just by experimenting with different Ks.

Valuing Houses in Seattle

Valuing houses in Seattle is a tough gamble. According to Zillow, their Zestimate is consistently off in Seattle. Regardless, how would we go about building something that tells us how valuable the houses are in Seattle? This section will walk through a simple example so that you can figure out with reasonable accuracy what a house is worth based on freely available data from the King County Assessor.

If you'd like to follow along in the code examples, check out the GitHub repo (*https:// github.com/thoughtfulml/examples-in-python/tree/master/k-nearest-neighbors*).

About the Data

While the data is freely available, it wasn't easy to put together. I did a bit of cajoling to get the data well formed. There's a lot of features, ranging from inadequate parking to whether the house has a view of Mount Rainier or not. I felt that while that was an interesting exercise, it's not really important to discuss here. In addition to the data they gave us, geolocation has been added to all of the datapoints so we can come up with a location distance much easier.

General Strategy

Our general strategy for finding the values of houses in Seattle is to come up with something we're trying to minimize/maximize so we know how good the model is. Since we will be looking at house values explicitly, we can't calculate an "Accuracy" rate because every value will be different. So instead we will utilize a different metric called *mean absolute error*.

With all models, our goal is to minimize or maximize something, and in this case we're going to minimize the mean absolute error. This is defined as the average of the absolute errors. The reason we'll use absolute error over any other common metrics (like mean squared error) is that it's useful. When it comes to house values it's hard to get intuition around the average squared error, but by using absolute error we can instead say that our model is off by $70,000 or similar on average.

As for unit testing and functional testing, we will approach this in a random fashion by stratifying the data into multiple chunks so that we can sample the mean absolute errors. This is mainly so that we don't find just one weird case where the mean absolute error was exceptionally low. We will not be talking extensively here about unit testing because this is an early chapter and I feel that it's more important to focus on the overall testing of the model through mean absolute error.

Coding and Testing Design

The basic design of the code for this chapter is going to center around a `Regressor` class. This class will take in King County housing data that comes in via a flat, calculate an error rate, and do the regression (Figure 3-13). We will not be doing any unit testing in this chapter but instead will visually test the code using the `plot_error` function we will build inside of the `Regressor` class.

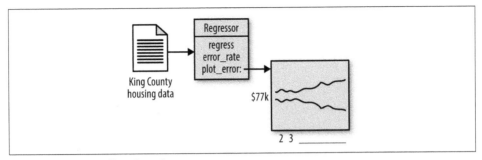

Figure 3-13. Overall coding design

For this chapter we will determine success by looking at the nuances of how our regressor works as we increase folds.

KNN Regressor Construction

To construct our KNN regression we will utilize something called a KDTree. It's not essential that you know how these work but the idea is the KDTree will store data in a easily queriable fashion based on distance. The distance metric we will use is the Euclidean distance since it's easy to compute and will suit us just fine. You could try many other metrics to see whether the error rate was better or worse.

A Note on Packages

You'll note that we're using quite a few packages. Python has excellent tools available to do anything data science related such as NumPy, Pandas, scikit-learn, SciPy, and others.

Pandas and NumPy work together to build what is at its core a multidimensional array but operates similar to an SQL database in that you can query it. Pandas is the query interface and NumPy is the numerical processing underneath. You will also find other useful tools inside of the NumPy library.

scikit-learn is a collection of machine learning tools available for common algorithms (that we will be talking about in this book).

SciPy is a scientific computing library that allows us to do things like use a KDTree.

As we progress in the book we will rely heavily on these libraries.

```
import random
import sys

import pandas as pd
import numpy as np
from scipy.spatial import KDTree
```

```
from sklearn.metrics import mean_absolute_error
import matplotlib.pyplot as plt

sys.setrecursionlimit(10000)

class Regression(object):
    """
    Performs kNN regression
    """

    def __init__(self):
        self.k = 5
        self.metric = np.mean
        self.kdtree = None
        self.houses = None
        self.values = None

    def set_data(self, houses, values):
        """
        Sets houses and values data
        :param houses: pandas.DataFrame with houses parameters
        :param values: pandas.Series with houses values
        """
        self.houses = houses
        self.values = values
        self.kdtree = KDTree(self.houses)
```

Do note that we had to set the recursion limit higher since KDTree will recurse and throw an error otherwise.

There's a few things we're doing here I thought we should discuss. One of them is the idea of normalizing data. This is a great trick to make all of the data similar. Otherwise, what will happen is that we find something close that really shouldn't be, or the bigger numbered dimensions will skew results.

On top of that we're only selecting latitude and longitude and SqFtLot, because this is a proof of concept.

```
class Regression(object):
    # __init__
    # set_data
    def regress(self, query_point):
        """
        Calculates predicted value for house with particular parameters
        :param query_point: pandas.Series with house parameters
        :return: house value
        """
        _, indexes = self.kdtree.query(query_point, self.k)
        value = self.metric(self.values.iloc[indexes])
        if np.isnan(value):
            raise Exception('Unexpected result')
```

```
    else:
        return value
```

Here we are querying the KDTree to find the closest K houses. We then use the metric, in this case mean, to calculate a regression value.

At this point we need to focus on the fact that, although all of this is great, we need some sort of test to make sure our data is working properly.

KNN Testing

Up until this point we've written a perfectly reasonable KNN regression tool to tell us house prices in King County. But how well does it actually perform? To do that we use something called cross-validation, which involves the following generalized algorithm:

- Take a training set and split it into two categories: testing and training
- Use the training data to train the model
- Use the testing data to test how well the model performs.

We can do that with the following code:

```
class RegressionTest(object):
    """
    Take in King County housing data, calculate and
    plot the kNN regression error rate.
    """

    def __init__(self):
        self.houses = None
        self.values = None

    def load_csv_file(self, csv_file, limit=None):
        """
        Loads CSV file with houses data
        :param csv_file: CSV file name
        :param limit: number of rows of file to read
        """
        houses = pd.read_csv(csv_file, nrows=limit)
        self.values = houses['AppraisedValue']
        houses = houses.drop('AppraisedValue', 1)
        houses = (houses - houses.mean()) / (houses.max() - houses.min())
        self.houses = houses
        self.houses = self.houses[['lat', 'long', 'SqFtLot']]

    def tests(self, folds):
        """
        Calculates mean absolute errors for series of tests
        :param folds: how many times split the data
        :return: list of error values
```

```
    """
    holdout = 1 / float(folds)
    errors = []
    for _ in range(folds):
      values_regress, values_actual = self.test_regression(holdout)
      errors.append(mean_absolute_error(values_actual, values_regress))

    return errors

  def test_regression(self, holdout):
    """
    Calculates regression for out-of-sample data
    :param holdout: part of the data for testing [0,1]
    :return: tuple(y_regression, values_actual)
    """
    test_rows = random.sample(self.houses.index.tolist(),
              int(round(len(self.houses) * holdout)))
    train_rows = set(range(len(self.houses))) - set(test_rows)
    df_test = self.houses.ix[test_rows]
    df_train = self.houses.drop(test_rows)

    train_values = self.values.ix[train_rows]
    regression = Regression()
    regression.set_data(houses=df_train, values=train_values)

    values_regr = []
    values_actual = []

    for idx, row in df_test.iterrows():
      values_regr.append(regression.regress(row))
      values_actual.append(self.values[idx])

    return values_regr, values_actual
```

Folds are generally how many times you wish to split the data. So for instance if we had 3 folds we would hold 2/3 of the data for training and 1/3 for testing and iterate through the problem set 3 times (Figure 3-14).

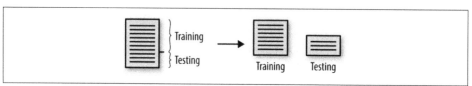

Figure 3-14. Split data into training and testing

Now these datapoints are interesting, but how well does our model perform? To do that, let's take a visual approach and write code that utilizes Pandas' graphics and matplotlib.

```python
class RegressionTest(object):
  # __init__
  # load_csv_file
  # tests
  # test_regression

  def plot_error_rates(self):
    """
    Plots MAE vs #folds
    """
    folds_range = range(2, 11)
    errors_df = pd.DataFrame({'max': 0, 'min': 0}, index=folds_range)
    for folds in folds_range:
      errors = self.tests(folds)
      errors_df['max'][folds] = max(errors)
      errors_df['min'][folds] = min(errors)
    errors_df.plot(title='Mean Absolute Error of KNN over different folds_range')
    plt.xlabel('#folds_range')
    plt.ylabel('MAE')
    plt.show()
```

We finally run this by running the following script:

```python
def main():
  regression_test = RegressionTest()
  regression_test.load_csv_file('king_county_data_geocoded.csv', 100)
  regression_test.plot_error_rates()


if __name__ == '__main__':
  main()
```

Running this yields the graph in Figure 3-15.

As you can see, starting with folds of 2 we have a fairly tight absolute deviation of about $77,000 dollars. As we increase the folds and, as a result, reduce the testing sample, that increases to a range of $73,000 to $77,000. For a very simplistic model that contains all information from waterfront property to condos, this actually does quite well!

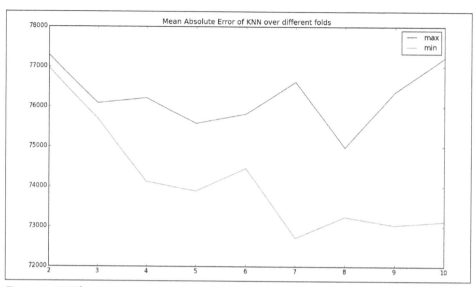

Figure 3-15. The error rates we achieved. The x-axis is the number of folds, and the y-axis is the absolute error in estimated home price (i.e., how much it's off by).

Conclusion

While K-Nearest Neighbors is a simple algorithm, it yields quite good results. We have seen that for distance-based problems we can utilize KNN to great effect. We also learned about how you can use this algorithm for either a classification or regression problem. We then analyzed the regression we built using a graphic representing the error.

Next, we showed that KNN has a downside that is inherent in any distance-based metric: the curse of dimensionality. This curse is something we can overcome using feature transformations or selections.

Overall it's a great algorithm and it stands the test of time.

## CHAPTER 4

Naive Bayesian Classification

Remember how email was several years ago? You probably recall your inbox being full of spam messages ranging from Nigerian princes wanting to pawn off money to pharmaceutical advertisements. It became such a major issue that we spent most of our time filtering spam.

Nowadays we spend a lot less time filtering spam than we used to, thanks to Gmail and tools like SpamAssassin. Using a method called a Naive Bayesian Classifier, such tools have been able to mitigate the influx of spam to our inboxes. This chapter will explore that topic as well as:

- Bayes' theorem
- What a Naive Bayesian Classifier is and why it's called "naive"
- How to build a spam filter using a Naive Bayesian Classifier

As noted in Table 2-2, a Naive Bayes Classifier is a supervised and probabilistic learning method. It does well with data in which the inputs are independent from one another. It also prefers problems where the probability of any attribute is greater than zero.

Using Bayes' Theorem to Find Fraudulent Orders

Imagine you're running an online store and lately you've been overrun with fraudulent orders. You estimate that about 10% of all orders coming in are fraudulent. In other words, in 10% of orders, people are stealing from you. Now of course you want to mitigate this by reducing the fraudulent orders, but you are facing a conundrum.

Every month you receive at least 1,000 orders, and if you were to check every single one, you'd spend more money fighting fraud than the fraud was costing you in the first place. Assuming that it takes up to 60 seconds per order to determine whether it's fraudulent or not, and a customer service representative costs around $15 per hour to hire, that totals 200 hours and $3,000 per year.

Another way of approaching this problem would be to construct a probability that an order is over 50% fraudulent. In this case, we'd expect the number of orders we'd have to look at to be much lower. But this is where things become difficult, because the only thing we can determine is the probability that it's fraudulent, which is 10%. Given that piece of information, we'd be back at square one looking at all orders because it's more probable that an order is not fraudulent!

Let's say that we notice that fraudulent orders often use gift cards and multiple promotional codes. Using this knowledge, how would we determine what is fraudulent or not—namely, how would we calculate the probability of fraud given that the purchaser used a gift card?

To answer for that, we first have to talk about conditional probabilities.

Conditional Probabilities

Most people understand what we mean by the probability of something happening. For instance, the probability of an order being fraudulent is 10%. That's pretty straightforward. But what about the probability of an order being fraudulent given that it used a gift card? To handle that more complicated case, we need something called a conditional probability, which is defined as follows:

Equation 4-1. Conditional probability

$$P(A|B) = \frac{P(A \cap B)}{P(B)}$$

Probability Symbols

Generally speaking, writing $P(E)$ means that you are looking at the probability of a given event. This event can be a lot of different things, including the event that A and B happened, the probability that A or B happened, or the probability of A given B happening in the past. Here we'll cover how you'd notate each of these scenarios.

$A \cap B$ is called the intersection function but could also be thought of as the Boolean operation AND. For instance, in Python it looks like this:

```
a = [1,2,3]
b = [1,4,5]

set(a) & set(b) #=> [1]
```

$A \cup B$ could be called the OR function, as it is both A and B. For instance, in Python it looks like the following:

```
a = [1,2,3]
b = [1,4,5]

set(a) | set(b) #=> [1,2,3,4,5]
```

Finally, the probability of A given B looks as follows in Python:

```
a = set([1,2,3])
b = set([1,4,5])

total = 5.0

p_a_cap_b = len(a & b) / total
p_b = len(b) / total

p_a_given_b = p_a_cap_b / p_b #=> 0.33
```

This definition basically says that the probability of A happening given that B happened is the probability of A and B happening divided by the probability of B. Graphically, it looks something like Figure 4-1.

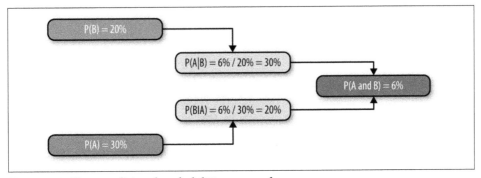

Figure 4-1. How conditional probabilities are made

This shows how $P(A \mid B)$ sits between $P(A \text{ and } B)$ and $P(B)$.

In our fraud example, let's say we want to measure the probability of fraud given that an order used a gift card. This would be:

$$P(Fraud \mid Giftcard) = \frac{P(Fraud \cap Giftcard)}{P(Giftcard)}$$

Now this works if you know the actual probability of Fraud and Giftcard.

At this point, we are up against the problem that we cannot calculate $P(Fraud \mid Giftcard)$ because that is hard to separate out. To solve this problem, we need to use a trick introduced by Bayes.

Inverse Conditional Probability (aka Bayes' Theorem)

In the 1700s, Reverend Thomas Bayes came up with the original research that would become Bayes' theorem. Pierre-Simon Laplace extended Bayes' research to produce the beautiful result we know today. Bayes' theorem is as follows:

Equation 4-2. Bayes' theorem

$$P(B \mid A) = \frac{P(A \mid B)P(B)}{P(A)}$$

This is because of the following:

Equation 4-3. Bayes' theorem expanded

$$P(B \mid A) = \frac{\frac{P(A \cap B)P(B)}{P(B)}}{P(A)} = \frac{P(A \cap B)}{P(A)}$$

This is useful in our fraud example because we can effectively back out our result using other information. Using Bayes' theorem, we would now calculate:

$$P(Fraud \mid Giftcard) = \frac{P(Giftcard \mid Fraud)P(Fraud)}{P(Giftcard)}$$

Remember that the probability of fraud was 10%. Let's say that the probability of gift card use is 10%, and based on our research the probability of gift card use in a fraudulent order is 60%. So what is the probability that an order is fraudulent given that it uses a gift card?

$$P(Fraud \mid Giftcard) = \frac{60\% \cdot 10\%}{10\%} = 60\%$$

The beauty of this is that your work on measuring fraudulent orders is drastically reduced because all you have to look for is the orders with gift cards. Because the total number of orders is 1,000, and 100 of those are fraudulent, we will look at 60 of those fraudulent orders. Out of the remaining 900, 90 used gift cards, which brings the total we need to look at to 150!

At this point, you'll notice we reduced the orders needing fraud review from 1,000 to 150 (i.e., 15% of the total). But can we do better? What about introducing something like people using multiple promo codes or other information?

Naive Bayesian Classifier

We've already solved the problem of finding fraudulent orders given that a gift card was used, but what about the problem of fraudulent orders given the fact that they have gift cards, or multiple promo codes, or other features? How would we go about that?

Namely, we want to solve the problem of $P(A \mid B, C) = ?$. For this, we need a bit more information and something called the chain rule.

The Chain Rule

If you think back to probability class, you might recall that the probability of A and B happening is the probability of B given A times the probability of A. Mathematically, this looks like $P(A \cap B) = P(B|A)P(A)$. This is assuming these events are not mutually exclusive. Using something called a joint probability, this smaller result transforms into the chain rule.

Joint probabilities are the probability that all the events will happen. We denote this by using $\cap$. The generic case of the chain rule is:

Equation 4-4. Chain rule

$$P(A_1, A_2, \cdots, A_n) = P(A_1)P(A_2 \mid A_1)P(A_3 \mid A_1, A_2) \cdots P(A_n|A_1, A_2, \cdots, A_{n-1})$$

This expanded version is useful in trying to solve our problem by feeding lots of information into our Bayesian probability estimates. But there is one problem: this can quickly evolve into a complex calculation using information we don't have, so we make one big assumption and act naive.

Naiveté in Bayesian Reasoning

The chain rule is useful for solving potentially inclusive problems, but we don't have the ability to calculate all of those probabilities. For instance, if we were to introduce multiple promos into our fraud example, then we'd have the following to calculate:

$$P(Fraud \mid Giftcard, Promos) = \frac{P(Giftcard, Promos \mid Fraud)P(Fraud)}{P(Giftcard, Promos)}$$

Let's ignore the denominator for now, as it doesn't depend on whether the order is fraudulent or not. At this point, we need to focus on finding the calculation for $P(Giftcard, Promos|Fraud)P(Fraud)$. If we apply the chain rule, this is equivalent to $P(Fraud, Giftcard, Promos)$.

You can see this by the following (note that *Fraud*, *Giftcard*, and *Promo* have been abbreviated for space):

$$P(F, G, P) = P(F)P(G, P | F)$$

$$P(F)P(G, P | F) = P(F)P(G | F)P(P | F, G)$$

Now at this point we have a conundrum: how do you measure the probability of a promo code given fraud and gift cards? While this is the correct probability, it really can be difficult to measure—especially with more features coming in. What if we were to be a tad naive and assume that we can get away with independence and just say that we don't care about the interaction between promo codes and gift cards, just the interaction of each independently with fraud?

In that case, our math would be much simpler:

$$P(Fraud, Giftcard, Promo) = P(Fraud)P(Giftcard | Fraud)P(Promo | Fraud)$$

This would be proportional to our numerator. And, to simplify things even more, we can assert that we'll normalize later with some magical Z, which is the sum of all the probabilities of classes. So now our model becomes:

$$P(Fraud | Giftcard, Promo) = \frac{1}{Z}P(Fraud)P(Giftcard | Fraud)P(Promo | Fraud)$$

To turn this into a classification problem, we simply determine which input—fraud or not fraud—yields the highest probability. See Table 4-1.

Table 4-1. Probability of gift cards versus promos

	Fraud	Not fraud
Gift card present	60%	30%
Multiple promos used	50%	30%
Probability of class	10%	90%

At this point, you can use this information to determine whether an order is fraudulent based purely on whether it has a gift card present and whether it used multiple promos. The probability that an order is fraudulent given the use of gift cards and multiple promos is 62.5%. While we can't exactly figure out how much savings this gives you in terms of the number of orders you must review, we know that we're using better information and making a better judgment.

There is one problem, though: what happens when the probability of using multiple promos given a fraudulent order is zero? A zero result can happen for several reasons, including that there just isn't enough of a sample size. The way we solve this is by using something called a pseudocount.

Pseudocount

There is one big challenge with a Naive Bayesian Classifier, and that is the introduction of new information. For instance, let's say we have a bunch of emails that are classified as spam or ham. We build our probabilities using all of this data, but then something bad happens: a new spammy word, fuzzbolt. Nowhere in our data did we see the word fuzzbolt, and so when we calculate the probability of spam given the word fuzzbolt, we get a probability of zero. This can have a zeroing-out effect that will greatly skew results toward the data we have.

Because a Naive Bayesian Classifier relies on multiplying all of the independent probabilities together to come up with a classification, if any of those probabilities are zero then our probability will be zero.

Take, for instance, the email subject "Fuzzbolt: Prince of Nigeria." Assuming we strip off *of*, we have the data shown in Table 4-2.

Table 4-2. Probability of word given ham or spam

Word	Spam	Ham
Fuzzbolt	0	0
Prince	75%	15%
Nigeria	85%	10%

Now let's assume we want to calculate a score for ham or spam. In both cases, the score would end up being zero because fuzzbolt isn't present. At that point, because we have a tie, we'd just go with the more common situation, which is ham. This means that we have failed and classified something incorrectly due to one word not being recognized.

There is an easy fix for that: pseudocount. When we go about calculating the probability, we add one to the count of the word. So, in other words, everything will end up being word_count + 1. This helps mitigate the zeroing-out effect for now. In the case of our fraud detector, we would add one to each count to ensure that it is never zero.

So in our preceding example, let's say we have 3,000 words. We would give fuzzbolt a score of $\frac{1}{3000}$. The other scores would change slightly, but this avoids the zeroing-out problem.

Spam Filter

The canonical machine learning example is building a spam filter. In this section, we will work up a simple spam filter, SpamTrainer, using a Naive Bayesian Classifier and improve it by utilizing a 3-gram tokenization model.

As you have learned before, Naive Bayesian Classifiers can be easily calculated, and operate well under strongly independent conditions. In this example, we will cover the following:

- What the classes look like interacting with each other
- A good data source
- A tokenization model
- An objective to minimize our error
- A way to improve over time

Setup Notes

Python is constantly changing and I have tried to keep the examples working under both 3.5.x and 2.7.x Python. That being said, things might change as Python changes. For more comprehensive information check out the GitHub repo (*https://github.com/ thoughtfulml/examples-in-python/tree/master/naive_bayes*).

Coding and Testing Design

In our example, each email has an object that takes an *.eml* type text file that then tokenizes it into something the SpamTrainer can utilize for incoming email messages. See Figure 4-2 for the class diagram.

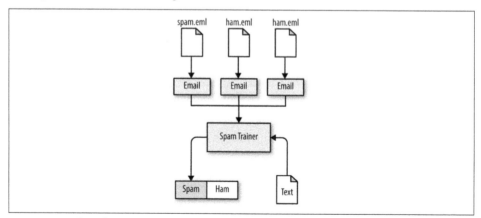

Figure 4-2. Class diagram showing how emails get turned into a SpamTrainer

When it comes to testing we will focus on the tradeoff between false positives and false negatives. With spam detection it becomes important to realize that a false positive (classifying an email as spam when it isn't) could actually be very bad for business. We will focus on minimizing the false positive rate but similar results could be applied to minimizing false negatives or having them equal each other.

Data Source

There are numerous sources of data that we can use, but the best is raw email messages marked as either spam or ham. For our purposes, we can use the CSDMC2010 SPAM corpus (*http://www.csmining.org/index.php/spam-email-datasets-.html*).

This data set has 4,327 total messages, of which 2,949 are ham and 1,378 are spam. For our proof of concept, this should work well enough.

EmailObject

The `EmailObject` class has one responsibility, which is to parse an incoming email message according to the RFC for emails. To handle this, we use the standard library in Python because there's a lot of nuance in there. In our model, all we're concerned with is subject and body.

The cases we need to handle are HTML messages, plaintext, and multipart. Everything else we'll just ignore. Building this class using test-driven development, let's go through this step by step.

Starting with the simple plaintext case, we'll copy one of the example training files from our data set under *data/TRAINING/TRAIN_00001.eml* to *./test/fixtures/plain.eml*. This is a plaintext email and will work for our purposes. Note that the split between a message and header in an email is usually denoted by "\r\n\r\n". Along with that header information is generally something like "Subject: A Subject goes here." Using that, we can easily extract our test case, which is:

```
import unittest

import io
import re
from naive_bayes.email_object import EmailObject


class TestPlaintextEmailObject(unittest.TestCase):
  CLRF = "\n\n"

  def setUp(self):
    self.plain_file = './tests/fixtures/plain.eml'
    with io.open(self.plain_file, 'rb') as plaintext:
      self.text = plaintext.read().decode('utf-8')
      plaintext.seek(0)
```

```
    self.plain_email = EmailObject(plaintext)

  def test_parse_plain_body(self):
    body = self.CLRF.join(self.text.split(self.CLRF)[1:])
    self.assertEqual(self.plain_email.body(), body)

  def test_parses_the_subject(self):
    subject = re.search("Subject: (.*)", self.text).group(1)
    self.assertEqual(self.plain_email.subject(), subject)
```

Unit Testing in Python

Up until this point we haven't introduced the unittest package in Python. Its main objective is to define unit tests for us to run on our code. Like similar unit testing frameworks in other languages like Ruby, we build a class that is prefixed with "Test" and then implement specific methods.

Methods to implement:

- Any method that is prefixed with `test_` will be treated as a test to be run.
- `setUp(self)` is a special method that gets run before any test gets run. Think of this like a block of code that gets run before all tests (Table 4-3).

Table 4-3. Python unittest has many assertions we can use

Method	Checks
assertEqual(a, b)	a == b
assertNotEqual(a, b)	a != b
assertTrue(x)	bool(x) is True
assertFalse(x)	bool(x) is False
assertIs(a,b)	a is b
assertIsNot(a,b)	a is not b
assertIsNone(x)	x is None
assertIsNotNone(x)	x is not None
assertIn(a,b)	a in b
assertNotIn(a,b)	a not in b
assertIsInstance(a,b)	isinstance(a,b)
assertNotIsInstance(a,b)	not isinstance(a,b)

Do note that we will not use all of these methods; they are listed here for future reference.

Now instead of relying purely on regular expressions, we'll use the standard library of Python. The standard library will handle all of the nitty-gritty details. Making email work for this particular case, we have:

```python
import email
import sys

from bs4 import BeautifulSoup


class EmailObject(object):
    """
    Parses incoming email messages
    """
    CLRF = "\n\r\n\r"

    def __init__(self, infile, category=None):
        self.category = category
        if sys.version_info > (3, 0):
            # Python 3 code in this block
            self.mail = email.message_from_binary_file(infile)
        else:
            # Python 2 code in this block
            self.mail = email.message_from_file(infile)

    def subject(self):
        """
        Get message subject line
        :return: str
        """
        return self.mail.get('Subject')

    def body(self):
        """
        Get message body
        :return: str in Py3, unicode in Py2
        """
        payload = self.mail.get_payload()
        return self._single_body(self.mail)

    @staticmethod
    def _single_body(part):
        """
        Get text from part.
        :param part: email.Message
        :return: str body or empty str if body cannot be decoded
        """
        content_type = part.get_content_type()
        try:
            body = part.get_payload(decode=True)
        except Exception:
            return ''
```

```
    return body
```

 BeautifulSoup is a library that parses HTML and XML.

Now that we have captured the case of plaintext, we need to solve the case of HTML. For that, we want to capture only the `inner_text`. But first we need a test case, which looks something like this:

```python
import unittest

import io
import re
from bs4 import BeautifulSoup
from naive_bayes.email_object import EmailObject

class TestHTMLEmail(unittest.TestCase):
  def setUp(self):
    with io.open('./tests/fixtures/html.eml', 'rb') as html_file:
      self.html = html_file.read().decode('utf-8')
      html_file.seek(0)
      self.html_email = EmailObject(html_file)

  def test_parses_stores_inner_text_html(self):
    body = "\n\n".join(self.html.split("\n\n")[1:])
    expected = BeautifulSoup(body, 'html.parser').text
    actual_body = self.html_email.body()
    self.assertEqual(actual_body, expected)

  def test_stores_subject(self):
    expected_subject = re.search("Subject: (.*)", self.html).group(1)
    actual_subject = self.html_email.subject()
    self.assertEqual(actual_subject, expected_subject)
```

As mentioned, we're using BeautifulSoup to calculate the `inner_text`, and we'll have to use it inside of the `Email` class as well. Now the problem is that we also need to detect the `content_type`. So we'll add that in:

```python
import email
import sys

from bs4 import BeautifulSoup


class EmailObject(object):

class EmailObject:
```

```
# __init__
# subject
# body

@staticmethod
def _single_body(part):
    """
    Get text from part.
    :param part: email.Message
    :return: str body or empty str if body cannot be decoded
    """
    content_type = part.get_content_type()
    try:
        body = part.get_payload(decode=True)
    except Exception:
        return ''

    if content_type == 'text/html':
        return BeautifulSoup(body, 'html.parser').text
    elif content_type == 'text/plain':
        return body
    return ''
```

At this point, we could add multipart processing as well, but I will leave that as an exercise that you can try out yourself. In the coding repository mentioned earlier in the chapter, you can see the multipart version.

Now we have a working email parser, but we still have to deal with tokenization, or what to extract from the body and subject.

Tokenization and Context

As Figure 4-3 shows, there are numerous ways to tokenize text, such as by stems, word frequencies, and words. In the case of spam, we are up against a tough problem because things are more contextual. The phrase *Buy now* sounds spammy, whereas *Buy* and *now* do not. Because we are building a Naive Bayesian Classifier, we are assuming that each individual token is contributing to the spamminess of the email.

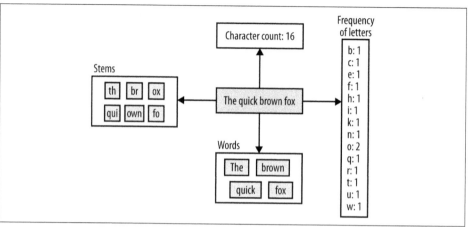

Figure 4-3. Lots of ways to tokenize text

The goal of the tokenizer we'll build is to extract words into a stream. Instead of returning an array, we want to yield the token as it happens so that we are keeping a low memory profile. Our tokenizer should also downcase all strings to keep them similar:

```python
import unittest

from naive_bayes.tokenizer import Tokenizer


class TestTokenizer(unittest.TestCase):
    def setUp(self):
        self.string = "this is a test of the emergency broadcasting system"

    def test_downcasing(self):
        expectation = ["this", "is", "all", "caps"]

        actual = Tokenizer.tokenize("THIS IS ALL CAPS")
        self.assertEqual(actual, expectation)

    def test_ngrams(self):
        expectation = [
            [u'\u0000', "quick"],
            ["quick", "brown"],
            ["brown", "fox"],
        ]

        actual = Tokenizer.ngram("quick brown fox", 2)
        self.assertEqual(actual, expectation)
```

As promised, we do two things in this tokenizer code. First, we lowercase all words. Second, instead of returning an array, we use a block. This is to mitigate memory constraints, as there is no need to build an array and return it. This makes it lazier. To make the subsequent tests work, though, we will have to fill in the skeleton for our tokenizer module like so:

```python
class Tokenizer:
  """
  Splits lines by whitespaces, converts to lower case and builds n-grams.
  """
  NULL = u'\u0000'

  @staticmethod
  def tokenize(string):
    return re.findall("\w+", string.lower())

  @staticmethod
  def unique_tokenizer(string):
    return set(Tokenizer.tokenize(string))

  @staticmethod
  def ngram(string, ngram):
    tokens = Tokenizer.tokenize(string)

    ngrams = []

    for i in range(len(tokens)):
      shift = i - ngram + 1
      padding = max(-shift, 0)
      first_idx = max(shift, 0)
      last_idx = first_idx + ngram - padding

      ngrams.append(Tokenizer.pad(tokens[first_idx:last_idx], padding))

    return ngrams

  @staticmethod
  def pad(tokens, padding):
    padded_tokens = []

    for i in range(padding):
      padded_tokens.append(Tokenizer.NULL)

    return padded_tokens + tokens
```

Now that we have a way of parsing and tokenizing emails, we can move on to build the Bayesian portion: the SpamTrainer.

SpamTrainer

The SpamTrainer will accomplish three things:

- Storing training data
- Building a Bayesian classifier
- Error minimization through cross-validation

Storing training data

The first step we need to tackle is to store training data from a given set of email messages. In a production environment, you would pick something that has persistence. In our case, we will go with storing everything in one big dictionary.

 A *set* is a unique collection of data.

Remember that most machine learning algorithms have two steps: training and then computation. Our training step will consist of these substeps:

- Storing a set of all categories
- Storing unique word counts for each category
- Storing the totals for each category

So first we need to capture all of the category names; that test would look something like this:

```
import unittest

import io
from naive_bayes.email_object import EmailObject
from naive_bayes.spam_trainer import SpamTrainer


class TestSpamTrainer(unittest.TestCase):
    def setUp(self):
        self.training = [['spam', './tests/fixtures/plain.eml'],
                         ['ham', './tests/fixtures/small.eml'],
                         ['scram', './tests/fixtures/plain.eml']]
        self.trainer = SpamTrainer(self.training)
        with io.open('./tests/fixtures/plain.eml', 'rb') as eml_file:
            self.email = EmailObject(eml_file)

    def test_multiple_categories(self):
        categories = self.trainer.categories
        expected = set([k for k, v in self.training])
        self.assertEqual(categories, expected)
```

The solution is in the following code:

```python
import io
from collections import defaultdict

from naive_bayes.tokenizer import Tokenizer
from naive_bayes.email_object import EmailObject


class SpamTrainer(object):
    """
    Storing training data
    Building a Bayesian classifier
    Error minimization through cross-validation
    """

    def __init__(self, training_files):
        self.categories = set()

        for category, _ in training_files:
            self.categories.add(category)

        self.totals = defaultdict(float)

        self.training = {c: defaultdict(float) for c in self.categories}

        self.to_train = training_files

    def total_for(self, category):
        """
        Get
        :param category:
        :return:
        """
        return self.totals[category]
```

You'll notice we're just using a set to capture this for now, as it'll hold on to the unique version of what we need. Our next step is to capture the unique tokens for each email. We are using the special category called _all to capture the count for everything:

```python
class TestSpamTrainer(unittest.TestCase):
    # setUp
    # test_multiple_categories

    def test_counts_all_at_zero(self):
        for cat in ['_all', 'spam', 'ham', 'scram']:
            self.assertEqual(self.trainer.total_for(cat), 0)
```

To get this to work, we have introduced a new method called train(), which will take the training data, iterate over it, and save it into an internal hash. The following is a solution:

```
class SpamTrainer(object):
  # __init__
  # total_for

  def train(self):
    for category, file in self.to_train:
      with io.open(file, 'rb') as eml_file:
        email = EmailObject(eml_file)

      self.categories.add(category)

      for token in Tokenizer.unique_tokenizer(email.body()):
        self.training[category][token] += 1
        self.totals['_all'] += 1
        self.totals[category] += 1

    self.to_train = {}
```

Now we have taken care of the training aspect of our program but really have no clue how well it performs. And it doesn't classify anything. For that, we still need to build our classifier.

Building the Bayesian classifier

To refresh your memory, Bayes' theorem is:

$$P(A_i \mid B) = \frac{P(B \mid A_i)P(A_i)}{\Sigma_j P(B \mid A_j)P(A_j)}$$

But because we're being naive about this, we've distilled it into something much simpler:

Equation 4-5. Bayesian spam score

$$Score(Spam, W_1, W_2, \cdots, W_n) = P(Spam)P(W_1 \mid Spam)P(W_2 \mid Spam)$$
$$\cdots P(W_n \mid Spam)$$

which is then divided by some normalizing constant, Z.

Our goal now is to build the methods `score`, `normalized_score`, and `classify`. The score method will just be the raw score from the preceding calculation, while `normalized_score` will fit the range from 0 to 1 (we get this by dividing by the total sum, Z).

The score method's test is as follows:

```
class TestSpamTrainer(unittest.TestCase):
  # setUp
  # test_multiple_categories
```

```
# test_counts_all_at_zero

def test_probability_being_1_over_n(self):
  trainer = self.trainer
  scores = list(trainer.score(self.email).values())

  self.assertAlmostEqual(scores[0], scores[-1])

  for i in range(len(scores) - 1):
    self.assertAlmostEqual(scores[i], scores[i + 1])
```

Because the training data is uniform across the categories, there is no reason for the score to differ across them. To make this work in our SpamTrainer object, we will have to fill in the pieces like so:

```
class SpamTrainer(object):
  # __init__
  # total_for
  # train

  def score(self, email):
    """
    Calculates score
    :param email: EmailObject
    :return: float number
    """
    self.train()

    cat_totals = self.totals

    aggregates = {cat: cat_totals[cat] / cat_totals['_all'] \
                  for cat in self.categories}

    for token in Tokenizer.unique_tokenizer(email.body()):
      for cat in self.categories:
        value = self.training[cat][token]
        r = (value + 1) / (cat_totals[cat] + 1)
        aggregates[cat] *= r

    return aggregates
```

This test does the following:

- First, it trains the model if it's not already trained (the train method handles this).
- For each token of the blob of an email we iterate through all categories and calculate the probability of that token being within that category. This calculates the Naive Bayesian score of each without dividing by Z.

Now that we have `score` figured out, we need to build a `normalized_score` that adds up to 1. Testing for this, we have:

```python
class TestSpamTrainer(unittest.TestCase):
  # setUp
  # test_multiple_categories
  # test_counts_all_at_zero
  # test_probability_being_1_over_n

  def test_adds_up_to_one(self):
    trainer = self.trainer
    scores = list(trainer.normalized_score(self.email).values())
    self.assertAlmostEqual(sum(scores), 1)
    self.assertAlmostEqual(scores[0], 1 / 2.0)
```

And subsequently on the `SpamTrainer` class we have:

```python
class SpamTrainer(object):
  # __init__
  # total_for
  # train
  # score


  def normalized_score(self, email):
    """
    Calculates normalized score
    :param email: EmailObject
    :return: float number
    """

    score = self.score(email)
    scoresum = sum(score.values())

    normalized = {cat: (aggregate / scoresum) \
                  for cat, aggregate in score.items()}
    return normalized
```

Calculating a classification

Because we now have a score, we need to calculate a classification for the end user to use. This classification should take the form of an object that returns `guess` and `score`. There is an issue of tie breaking here.

Let's say, for instance, we have a model that has turkey and tofu. What happens when the scores come back evenly split? Probably the best course of action is to go with which is more popular, whether it be turkey or tofu. What about the case where the probability is the same? In that case, we can just go with alphabetical order.

When testing for this, we need to introduce a preference order—that is, the occurrence of each category. A test for this would be:

```
class TestSpamTrainer(unittest.TestCase):
  # setUp
  # test_multiple_categories
  # test_counts_all_at_zero
  # test_probability_being_1_over_n
  # test_adds_up_to_one

  def test_preference_category(self):
    trainer = self.trainer
    expected = sorted(trainer.categories,
                      key=lambda cat: trainer.total_for(cat))

    self.assertEqual(trainer.preference(), expected)
```

Getting this to work is trivial and would look like this:

```
class SpamTrainer(object):
  # __init__
  # total_for
  # train
  # score
  # normalized_score

  def preference(self):
    return sorted(self.categories, key=lambda cat: self.total_for(cat))
```

Now that we have `preference` set up, we can test for our classification being correct. The code to do that is as follows:

```
class TestSpamTrainer(unittest.TestCase):
  # setUp
  # test_multiple_categories
  # test_counts_all_at_zero
  # test_probability_being_1_over_n
  # test_adds_up_to_one
  # test_preference_category

  def test_give_preference_to_whatever_has_the_most(self):
    trainer = self.trainer
    score = trainer.score(self.email)

    preference = trainer.preference()[-1]
    preference_score = score[preference]

    expected = SpamTrainer.Classification(preference, preference_score)
    self.assertEqual(trainer.classify(self.email), expected)
```

Getting this to work in code again is simple:

```
class SpamTrainer:
  # __init__
  # total_for
  # train
  # score
```

```
# normalized_score
# preference

class Classification(object):
    """
    Guess and score
    """

    def __init__(self, guess, score):
        self.guess = guess
        self.score = score

    def __eq__(self, other):
        return self.guess == other.guess and self.score == other.score

def classify(self, email):
    score = self.score(email)

    max_score = 0.0
    preference = self.preference()
    max_key = preference[-1]

    for k, v in score.items():
        if v > max_score:
            max_key = k
            max_score = v
        elif v == max_score and preference.index(k) > preference.index(max_key):
            max_key = k
            max_score = v
    return self.Classification(max_key, max_score)
```

Error Minimization Through Cross-Validation

At this point, we need to measure how well our model works. To do so, we need to take the data that we downloaded earlier and do a cross-validation test on it. From there, we need to measure only false positives, and then based on that determine whether we need to fine-tune our model more.

Minimizing false positives

Up until this point, our goal with making models has been to minimize error. This error could be easily denoted as the count of misclassifications divided by the total classifications. In most cases, this is exactly what we want, but in a spam filter this isn't what we're optimizing for. Instead, we want to minimize false positives. False positives, also known as Type I errors, are when the model incorrectly predicts a positive when it should have been negative.

In our case, if our model predicts spam when in fact the email isn't, then the user will lose her emails. We want our spam filter to have as few false positives as possible. On the other hand, if our model incorrectly predicts something as ham when it isn't, we don't care as much.

Instead of minimizing the total misclassifications divided by total classifications, we want to minimize spam misclassifications divided by total classifications. We will also measure false negatives, but they are less important because we are trying to reduce spam that enters someone's mailbox, not eliminate it.

To accomplish this, we first need to take some information from our data set, which we'll cover next.

Building the two folds

Inside the spam email training data is a file called *keyfile.label*. It contains information about whether the file is spam or ham. Using that, we can build a cross-validation script. First let's start with setup, which involves importing the packages we've worked on and some IO and regular expression libraries:

```
import io

from spam_trainer import SpamTrainer
from email_object import EmailObject

print("Cross Validation")

correct = 0
false_positives = 0.0
false_negatives = 0.0
confidence = 0.0
```

This doesn't do much yet except start with a zeroed counter for correct, false positives, false negatives, and confidence. To set up the test we need to load the label data and turn that into a SpamTrainer object. We can do that using the following:

```
def label_to_training_data(fold_file):
  training_data = []

  for line in io.open(fold_file, 'r'):
    label_file = line.rstrip().split(' ')
    training_data.append(label_file)

  print(training_data)
  return SpamTrainer(training_data)

trainer = label_to_training_data('./tests/fixtures/fold1.label')
```

This instantiates a trainer object by calling the label_to_training_data function. Next we parse the emails we have in fold number 2:

```
def parse_emails(keyfile):
  emails = []
```

```
    print("Parsing emails for " + keyfile)

    for line in io.open(keyfile, 'r'):
      label, file = line.rstrip().split(' ')

      with io.open(file, 'rb') as eml_file:
        emails.append(EmailObject(eml_file, category=label))

    print("Done parsing files for " + keyfile)
    return emails

  emails = parse_emails('./tests/fixtures/fold2.label')
```

Now we have a trainer object and emails parsed. All we need to do now is calculate the accuracy and validation metrics:

```
def validate(trainer, set_of_emails):
  correct = 0
  false_positives = 0.0
  false_negatives = 0.0
  confidence = 0.0

  for email in set_of_emails:
    classification = trainer.classify(email)
    confidence += classification.score

    if classification.guess == 'spam' and email.category == 'ham':
      false_positives += 1
    elif classification.guess == 'ham' and email.category == 'spam':
      false_negatives += 1
    else:
      correct += 1

  total = false_positives + false_negatives + correct

  false_positive_rate = false_positives / total
  false_negative_rate = false_negatives / total
  accuracy = (false_positives + false_negatives) / total
  message = """
False Positives: {0}
False Negatives: {1}
Accuracy: {2}
""".format(false_positive_rate, false_negative_rate, accuracy)
  print(message)


  validate(trainer, emails)
```

Last, we can analyze the other direction of the cross-validation (i.e., validating fold1 against a fold2 trained model):

```
trainer = label_to_training_data('./tests/fixtures/fold2.label')
emails = parse_emails('./tests/fixtures/fold1.label')
validate(trainer, emails)
```

Cross-validation and error measuring

From here, we can actually build our cross-validation test, which will read fold1 and fold2 and then cross-validate to determine the actual error rate. The test looks something like this (see Table 4-4 for the results):

```
Cross Validation::Fold1 unigram model
    validates fold1 against fold2 with a unigram model

        False Positives: 0.0036985668053629217
        False Negatives: 0.16458622283865001
        Error Rate: 0.16828478964401294

Cross Validation::Fold2 unigram model
    validates fold2 against fold1 with a unigram model

        False Positives: 0.005545286506469501
        False Negatives: 0.17375231053604437
        Error Rate: 0.17929759704251386
```

Table 4-4. Spam versus ham

Category	Email count	Word count	Probability of email	Probability of word
Spam	1,378	231,472	31.8%	36.3%
Ham	2,949	406,984	68.2%	63.7%
Total	4,327	638,456	100%	100%

As you can see, ham is more probable, so we will default to that and more often than not we'll classify something as ham when it might not be. The good thing here, though, is that we have reduced spam by 80% without sacrificing incoming messages.

Conclusion

In this chapter, we have delved into building and understanding a Naive Bayesian Classifier. As you have learned, this algorithm is well suited for data that can be asserted to be independent. Being a probablistic model, it works well for classifying data into multiple directions given the underlying score. This supervised learning method is useful for fraud detection, spam filtering, and any other problem that has these types of features.

## CHAPTER 5

Decision Trees and Random Forests

Every day we make decisions. Every second we make decisions. Our perceptive brains receive roughly 12.5 gigabytes to 2.5 terabytes of information per second—an impressive amount—but they only focus on 60 bits of information per second.[1] Humans are exceptionally adept at taking in lots of data and quickly finding patterns in it.

But we're not so great under pressure. In Chapter 1 we discussed flight and how checklists have solved many of its problems. We don't use checklists because we're stupid; on the contrary, it's because under stress we forget small bits of information.

What if the effects of our decisions were even greater? Take, for instance, classifying mushrooms in the forest. If you are lucky enough to live in a climate that supports mushrooms such as morels, which are delicious, then you can see the allure of going to find your own, as they are quite expensive! But as we all know finding mushrooms in the forest is extremely dangerous if you misclassify them.

While death by mushroom is quite rare, the effects are well documented. Death caps, *Amanita phalloides*, cause liver failure. On the other hand, if you were to eat a *Psilocybe semilanceata* by accident, you would be in for a trip. Also known as liberty caps, these are the notorious magic mushrooms that people ingest to experience psychedelic effects!

While we as humans are good at processing information, we might not be the best at making decisions that are objective. When our decisions can produce outcomes as

---

1 "New Measure of Human Brain Processing Speed," *MIT Technology Review*, August 25, 2009, *http://bit.ly/new-measure-brain*; James Randerson, "How Many Neurons Make a Human Brain? Billions Fewer Than We Thought," *The Guardian*, February 28, 2012, *http://bit.ly/how-many-neurons*; AI Impacts, "Neuron Firing Rates in Humans," April 4, 2014, *http://aiimpacts.org/rate-of-neuron-firing/*.

varied as a psychedelic high, death, or delicious food, we need to apply an algorithm. For that we'll use decision trees.

 This should never be used to find mushrooms in the woods. Don't do it, ever, unless you are a trained mycologist or traveling with an experienced mycologist. You risk a terrible death if you do so. This is purely educational and should only be used to see the nuances between mushrooms as well as understand our fungus friends better.

In this chapter we will first talk about the nuances of mushrooms and how we will go about defining success with our model. We'll first take a fairly folk-theorem approach to classifying mushrooms using some of the normal classification techniques to determine whether something is poisonous or not. Then we'll move into splitting our data into pieces based on the attributes of mushrooms. We'll also talk about the ill effects of a deep tree.

Last, we'll discuss finding trees using an ensemble method called random forests. Throughout this chapter we will talk about how to approach this problem with a testing focus.

The Nuances of Mushrooms

As with any machine learning problem, knowing your domain is important. This domain knowledge can make or break many models and mushrooms are no different. These amazing fungi are hard to classify because similar-looking species can have vastly different effects when eaten. For instance in the *Boletus* genus there are *Boletus badius* (bay bolete), *Boletus pulcherrimus*, and *Boletus manicus* (see Figure 5-1).

Figure 5-1. Boletus badius and Boletus pulcherrimus. Source: Wikimedia.

The bay bolete is edible and delicious, *Boletus pulcherrimus* is poisonous, and *Boletus manicus* is psychedelic. They all look fairly similar since they are big fat mushrooms that share a common top.

If our goal was to find bolete-like mushrooms then we might find ourself in extreme danger. So what should we do? People have been classifying mushrooms for a long time and this has led to folk traditions.

Classifying Mushrooms Using a Folk Theorem

Folk traditions have led to a few heuristics we could use to build a model to help us classify mushrooms:

- Poisonous mushrooms are brightly colored.
- Insects and animals will avoid contact with poisonous mushrooms.
- Poisonous mushrooms will turn rice red if boiled.
- Poisonous mushrooms have a pointed cap. Edible mushrooms have a flat cap.
- Poisonous mushrooms taste bad.
- Boletes are safe to eat.[2]

All of these are erroneous and unfortunately have killed people who followed some of them. But we might be able to increase the accuracy of this list by bringing them all into one unified theorem or folk theorem.

Say, for instance, we first asked whether the mushroom was brightly colored or not, then asked whether insects or animals will avoid mushrooms, and so forth. We could keep asking questions until we find ourselves with a generalized answer.

Visually we could represent this as a flow chart (Figure 5-2).

But this is a loose way of building a model and suffers from the fact that we don't have data. As a matter of fact, I wouldn't condone collecting information on whether the mushroom tasted bad—that just seems dangerous. So what can we do instead?

---

2 For more information on mushrooms see Ian Robert Hall (2003), *Edible and Poisonous Mushrooms of the World* (Timber Press), p. 103, ISBN 0-88192-586-1.

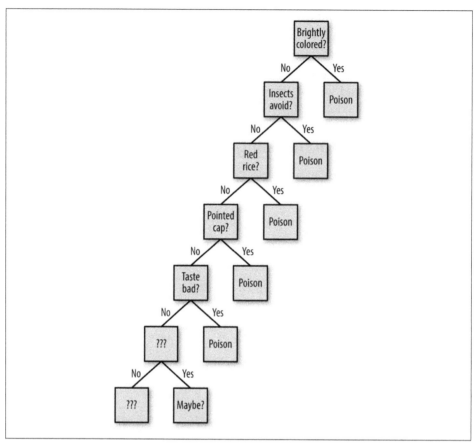

Figure 5-2. Folk theorem flow chart

Finding an Optimal Switch Point

Instead of focusing on domain knowledge, we could take a step back and focus on hard data. There is a data set that the University of California, Irvine owns about edible and poisonous mushrooms. Sorry, there's no information on psychedelic mushrooms in this data, but we can still use the data to come up with a better approach than the folk theorem.

The data contains quite a few attributes that might help us determine whether a mushroom is edible or not, such as cap shape, odor, and veil color. Instead of relying on folktales about what makes a mushroom poisonous or not, what does the data say?

We could, for instance, come up with a probability of each feature adding independently to the overall poisonousness of a mushroom. This would be a Naive Bayesian Classification but has the problem that each feature isn't independent. There is crossover. Maybe a mushroom that is bright and flat is okay to eat while a mushroom that is bright and round isn't.

Instead, to build this decision tree we can take the overall algorithm:

- Split data into subcategories using the most informational attribute.
- Keep going until threshold.

This algorithm is quite simple. The idea is to take the entire population of mushrooms, and split them into subcategories until we have a tree showing us how to classify something (Figure 5-3).

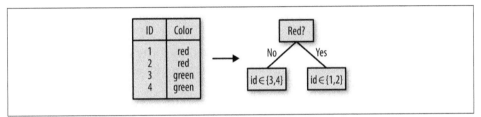

Figure 5-3. Splitting data using categories

Three common metrics are used to split data into subcategories:

1. Information gain
2. GINI impurity
3. Variance reduction

Information Gain

Knowing that our goal is to split a population of mushrooms into subcategories, we would want to split on attributes that improve our model. We want to take an attribute such as odor and determine how that affects the classification accuracy. This can be done using information gain.

Conceptually this is a metric of information theory and tells us how well the attribute tracks with the overall goal. It can be calculated as $Gain = H_{new} - H_{previous} = H(T) - H(T \mid a)$. This tells us the relative information entropy gain in positive terms. So for instance if the previous entropy was –2 and the new entropy is –1 then we would have a gain of 1.

Information theory primer: entropy is used as a way of determining just how descriptive bits are. A canonical example of entropy would be that if it's always sunny in Death Valley with a probability of 100% then the entropy would be 0 to send information about what the weather of the day was. The information doesn't need to be encoded since there's nothing to report.

Another example of high entropy would be having a complex password. The more numerous and diverse the characters you use, the higher the entropy. The same is true of attributes. If we have lots of possibilities for mushroom odor, then that would have higher entropy.

GINI Impurity

Not to be confused with the GINI coefficient, GINI impurity is a probabilistic measure. It defines how probable an attribute is at showing up and the probability of it being mistaken.

The formula for impurity is:

$$I_G(f) = \Sigma_{i=1}^{m} p(f_i)(1 - p(f_i)) = 1 - \Sigma_{i=1}^{m} p(f_i)^2$$

To understand this, examine a person's simple taste profile (Table 5-1).

Table 5-1. Taste profile

Like/Not Like	Sweet	Salty
Like	True	True
Like	True	False
Like	False	True
Not Like	False	False
Not Like	False	True

Measuring what the GINI impurity is for the factors "Sweet" and "Salty" would be calculated this way: sum the probability of that factor in a given class (Like/Not Like) over each factor (Sweet/Salty).

For instance with "Sweet":

$$I_G(Sweet) = \frac{2}{3}\left(1 - \frac{2}{3}\right) + \frac{0}{2}\left(1 - \frac{0}{2}\right) = \frac{2}{9}$$

Similarly:

$$I_G(Salty) = \frac{2}{3}\left(1 - \frac{2}{3}\right) + \frac{1}{2}\left(1 - \frac{1}{2}\right) = \frac{2}{9} + \frac{1}{4} = \frac{17}{36}$$

What this means is that the GINI impurity for Salty is higher than the GINI impurity for Sweet. Intuitively while creating a decision tree we would want to choose Sweet as a split point first, since it will create less impurity in the tree.

Variance Reduction

Variance reduction is used primarily in continuous decision trees. Conceptually variance reduction aims to reduce the dispersion of the classification. While it doesn't apply to classification problems such as whether mushrooms are edible or not, it does apply to continuous outputs. If, for instance, we would rather have a model that predicts in a predictable fashion:

$$\xi = E\left(X_{1j}\right) - E\left(X_{2j}\right) = \mu_1 - \mu_2$$

Decision trees are wonderful but have a major drawback: sometimes they overfit data. As we will see in many chapters in this book, overfitting is a big problem. We want to model our problem without memorizing the data. To solve this we need to figure out a way of making our model general. We do that through pruning.

Pruning Trees

When building a model to understand the nuances of mushrooms, we don't want to just memorize everything. While I highly suggest memorizing all the data for perfect classifications if you do forage for mushrooms, in this case we need to focus on the model of the mushroom kingdom. To build a better model we can use pruning.

Decision trees are NP in that they are generally hard to compute but easy to verify. This is even more amplified by the problem of complex trees. Our goal for pruning is to find a subtree of the full decision tree using the preceding decision points that minimizes this error surface:

$$\frac{err(prune(T,t),S) - err(T,S)}{|leaves(T)| - |leaves(prune(T,t))|}$$

Finding the optimal pruned tree is difficult because we need to run through all possibilities to find out which subtree is the best. To overcome this we need to rethink our original approach for training the decision tree in the first place. For that we'll utilize an ensemble method called random forests.

Ensemble Learning

We haven't discussed ensemble learning yet but it's a highly valuable tool in any machine learning programmer's toolkit. Ensemble methods are like meta-programming for machine learning. The basic idea is to build a model full of many submodels.

With our mushroom classification model we have discovered that we can find a solution but it takes a long time to run. We want to find the optimal subtree that can also be thought of as a decision tree that satisfies our model.

There are lots of ensemble methods, but for this chapter we will focus on bagging and random forests.

Bagging

One simple approach to ensemble learning is bagging, which is short for "bootstrap aggregation." This method was invented as a way to improve a model without changing anything except the training set. It does this by aggregating multiple random versions of the training set.

Imagine that we randomly sample data in our data set. For instance, we take a subset that overlooks something like the poisonous *Bolete* mushroom. For each one of these subsamples we train a decision tree using our metrics like the GINI impurity or information gain (Figure 5-4). For each of these models we then have an accuracy, precision, and recall associated with each.

Accuracy, precision, and recall are all metrics to determine how viable the model is that we have built. Many of us already know accuracy but haven't ran into precision or recall yet.

The definitions of each of these metrics are:

- Precision = True Positives / (True Positives + False Positives)
- Recall = True Positives / (True Positives + False Negatives)
- Accuracy = (True Positives + True Negatives) / (Number of all responses)

Precision is a measure of how on point the classification is. For instance, out of all the positive matches the model finds, how many of them were correct?

Recall can be thought of as the sensitivity of the model. It is a measure of whether all the relevant instances were actually looked at.

Accuracy as we know it is simply an error rate of the model. How well does it do in aggregate?

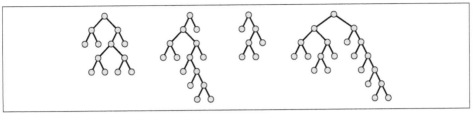

Figure 5-4. Many trees make up a random forest

We now have a set of decision trees that we can aggregate by finding the majority vote of a classification (Figure 5-5).

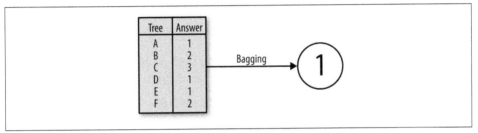

Figure 5-5. Voting usually is about picking the winner

This drastically improves performance because it reduces variability in the prediction but doesn't have a bunch of bias mixed in. What this implicitly means is that one decision tree will have a lot of noise contained within it, whereas decision trees in aggregate average out. This is similar to the central limit theorem.

Random forests

Another method to aggregating tree models together is to randomly select feature spaces. For instance in our mushroom kingdom we can build decision trees using five subfeatures at each iteration. This would yield at most 26,334 combinations (22 choose 5). What is intriguing is that we might find more information about our mushroom kingdom using this because some features might be more collaborative than others. Like bagging we can take the data and aggregate by votes.

> We will be discussing variable importance in a later chapter, but what is fascinating about decision trees is you can determine what is an important variable and use this to build features.

Writing a Mushroom Classifier

 For access to all the code contained in this chapter, visit the GitHub repo   (*https://github.com/thoughtfulml/examples-in-python/tree/master/decision_trees*).

Getting back to our example: what if we were to build something that classifies mushrooms into poisonous or edible based on the various features associated with them? There's an infinite amount of algorithms we could choose, but since we want something that's easy to understand, decision trees are a good candidate.

Coding and testing design

To build this mushroom classifier and regression we have to first build some classes. The basic idea is to feed in mushroom data that has attributes and whether it's edible.

From here we define the following classes (see Figure 5-6):

MushroomProblem
:   Implements `validation_data` for our use in validating the model

MushroomRegression
:   Implements a regression tree

MushroomClassifier
:   A utility class for classification problems

MushroomForrest
:   An implementation of random forests to classify mushrooms

MushroomTree
:   An implementation of a decision tree to classify mushrooms

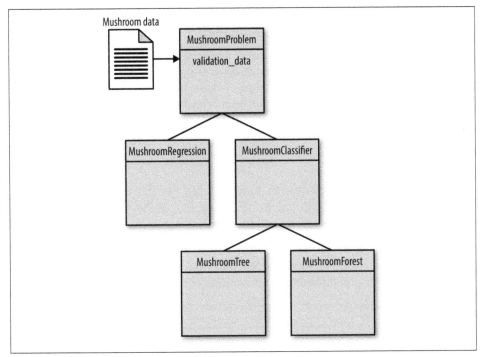

Figure 5-6. Class design for mushroom problem

Testing mushroom classification and regression will take two different forms: square error (for regression) and confusion matrices (Figure 5-7). Confusion matrices are a way of determining how well classification problems work.

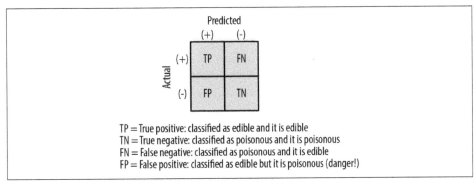

Figure 5-7. Confusion matrix example with yes or no answers

Confusion Matrix

Confusion matrices are a way of tabulating how well the classifier works. Given two categories, we want to test whether our classifier is right. Reading confusion matrices involves looking at actual and predicted pairs (down the diagonal) for what are classified as true classifications. For finding incorrect classifications, any actual and predicted column row pairs that don't match are incorrect classifications.

MushroomProblem

To write this classifier we first need to do some setup. For this we will rely on Pandas, NumPy, and scikit-learn. You'll notice that we use a lot of Pandas functions that help put the data into easy-to-use classes and features.

Let's start by defining the problem. Given a datafile of mushroom training data with attributes attached to it, we want to load that into a class that will factorize those attributes into numerical information and output validation data for testing:

```python
from sklearn.ensemble import RandomForestClassifier
from sklearn.tree import DecisionTreeClassifier, DecisionTreeRegressor
from numpy.random import permutation
from numpy import array_split, concatenate
from sklearn.metrics import mean_squared_error
import pandas as pd
import numpy as np

class MushroomProblem(object):
    """
    Mushrooms classification problem
    """

    def __init__(self, data_file):
        """
        Loads data file and prepares data
        :param data_file: CSV file name
        """
        self.data_frame = pd.read_csv(data_file)
        for k in self.data_frame.columns[1:]:
            self.data_frame[k], _ = pd.factorize(self.data_frame[k])

        categories = sorted(pd.Categorical(self.data_frame['class']).categories)
        self.classes = np.array(categories)
        self.features = self.data_frame.columns[self.data_frame.columns != 'class']

    @staticmethod
    def __factorize(data):
        y, _ = pd.factorize(pd.Categorical(data['class']), sort=True)
        return y
```

This sets up the initial class but then we also need a function that outputs a subset of data by having a variable amount of folds:

```python
class MushroomProblem(object):
    # __init__

    def validation_data(self, folds):
        """
        Performs data splitting, classifier training and prediction for given #folds
        :param folds: number of folds
        :return: list of numpy.array pairs (prediction, expected)
        """
        df = self.data_frame
        response = []

        assert len(df) > folds

        perms = array_split(permutation(len(df)), folds)

        for i in range(folds):
            train_idxs = list(range(folds))
            train_idxs.pop(i)
            train = []
            for idx in train_idxs:
                train.append(perms[idx])

            train = concatenate(train)

            test_idx = perms[i]

            training = df.iloc[train]
            test_data = df.iloc[test_idx]

            y = self.__factorize(training)
            classifier = self.train(training[self.features], y)
            predictions = classifier.predict(test_data[self.features])

            expected = self.__factorize(test_data)
            response.append([predictions, expected])

        return response
```

This first defines the problem we're trying to solve (i.e., the mushroom classification problem). From here we can take a few different approaches:

- A regression
- A classifier
  - Decision tree
  - Random forest

The major difference between them would be how the training method is set up. For instance, with a regression we'd just need:

```python
class MushroomRegression(MushroomProblem):
    """
    Implementation if mushrooms classification problem
    with sklearn.DecisionTreeRegressor
    """

    def train(self, X, Y):
        """
        Train classifier.
        :param X: training input samples
        :param Y: target values
        :return: regressor
        """
        regressor = DecisionTreeRegressor()
        regressor = regressor.fit(X, Y)
        return regressor

    def validate(self, folds):
        """
        Evaluate classifier using mean squared error
        :param folds: number of folds
        :return: list of MSE per fold
        """
        responses = []

        for y_true, y_pred in self.validation_data(folds):
            responses.append(mean_squared_error(y_true, y_pred))

        return responses
```

For our classifiers we can define them as such:

```python
class MushroomClassifier(MushroomProblem):
    """
    Partial implementation of mushrooms classification problem
    """

    def validate(self, folds):
        """
        Evaluate classifier using confusion matrices
        :param folds: number of folds
        :return: list of confusion matrices per fold
        """
        confusion_matrices = []

        for test, training in self.validation_data(folds):
            confusion_matrices.append(self.confusion_matrix(training, test))

        return confusion_matrices
```

```
    @staticmethod
    def confusion_matrix(train, test):
        return pd.crosstab(test, train, rownames=['actual'], colnames=['preds'])

class MushroomForest(MushroomClassifier):
    """
    Implementation of mushrooms classification problem
    with sklearn.RandomForestClassifier
    """

    def train(self, X, Y):
        """
        Train classifier.
        :param X: training input samples
        :param Y: target values
        :return: classifier
        """
        classifier = RandomForestClassifier(n_jobs=2)
        classifier = classifier.fit(X, Y)
        return classifier

class MushroomTree(MushroomClassifier):
    """
    Implementation of mushrooms classification problem
    with sklearn.DecisionTreeClassifier
    """

    def train(self, X, Y):
        """
        Train classifier.
        :param X: training input samples
        :param Y: target values
        :return: classifier
        """
        classifier = DecisionTreeClassifier()
        classifier = classifier.fit(X, Y)
        return classifier
```

While this is great, it doesn't really answer the question of how you would go about testing this. How good would this model really hold up?

Testing

The best testing method is to stratify our data into cross-validation folds and determine whether we are classifying properly. Otherwise we will output a mean squared error.

To do this we need some simple code to check:

```
from classifier import MushroomTree, MushroomForest, MushroomRegression

data = './data/agaricus-lepiota.data'
```

```
folds = 5

print("Calculating score for decision tree")

tree = MushroomTree(data)
print(tree.validate(folds))

print("Calculating score for random forest method")

forest = MushroomForest(data)
print(forest.validate(folds))

print("Calculating score for regression tree")

regression = MushroomRegression(data)
print(regression.validate(folds))
```

Running this code shows the following output. In the code, `actual` is the data inside of the training set. This is the data we hold to be true. `preds` are results we got out of the model we built:

```
Calculating score for decision tree
[preds      0    1
actual
0        844    0
1          0  781,
preds      0    1
actual
0        834    0
1          0  791,
preds      0    1
actual
0        814    0
1          0  811,
preds      0    1
actual
0        855    0
1          0  770,
preds      0    1
actual
0        861    0
1          0  763]
Calculating score for random forest method
[preds      0    1
actual
0        841    0
1          0  784,
preds      0    1
actual
0        869    0
1          0  756,
preds      0    1
```

```
actual
0          834    0
1            0   791,
preds        0    1
actual
0          835    0
1            0   790,
preds        0    1
actual
0          829    0
1            0   795]
Calculating score for regression tree
[0.0, 0.0, 0.0, 0.0, 0.0]
```

What you'll notice is, given this toy example, we are able to create a decision tree that does exceptionally well. Does that mean we should go out to the woods and eat mushrooms? No, but given the training data and information we gathered, we have built a highly accurate model of mapping mushrooms to either poisonous or edible!

The resulting decision tree is actually quite fascinating as you can see in Figure 5-8.

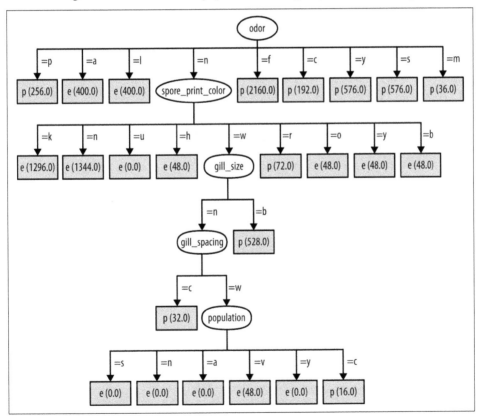

Figure 5-8. The resulting tree from building decision trees

I don't think it's important to discuss what this tree means, but it is interesting to think of mushroom poisonousness as a function of a handful of decision nodes.

Conclusion

In this chapter we learned how to classify data by using decision trees. This can be useful for making hierarchical classifications and when certain attributes determine split points well. We showed that decision trees and random forests are both well suited for classifying mushroom edibility. And remember—don't use this in the wild to classify mushrooms! Find a mycologist.

## CHAPTER 6

Hidden Markov Models

Intuition informs much of what we do: for example, it tells us that certain words tend to be a certain part of speech, or that if a user visits a signup page, she has a higher probability of becoming a customer. But how would you build a model around intuition?

Hidden Markov models (HMMs) are well versed in finding a *hidden state* of a given system using observations and an assumption about how those states work. In this chapter, we will first talk about how to track user states given their actions, then explore more about what an HMM is, and finally build a part-of-speech tagger using the Brown Corpus. The part-of-speech tagger will tag words in sentences as nouns, pronouns, or any part of speech in the Brown Corpus.

HMMs can be either supervised or unsupervised and also are called *Markovian* due to their reliance on a Markov model. They work well where there doesn't need to be a lot of historical information built into the model. They also work well for adding localized context to a classification. Unlike what we saw with Naive Bayesian Classification, which relied on a lot of history to determine whether a user is spammy or not, HMMs can be used to predict changes over time in a model.

Tracking User Behavior Using State Machines

Have you ever heard of the sales funnel? This is the idea that there are different levels of customer interaction. People will start as prospects and then transition into more engaged states (see Figure 6-1).

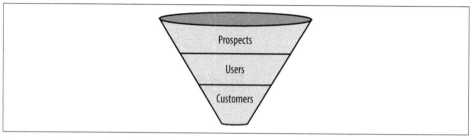

Figure 6-1. A generalized sales funnel

Prospects are "lurkers" who visit the site once or twice but usually don't engage. Users, on the other hand, like to browse and occasionally make purchases. Customers are quite engaged and have bought something but usually don't buy a lot in a short time, and thus go back to being users temporarily.

Let's say that we have an online store and determine that out of prospects that visit the site, 15% will sign up, and 5% will become customers right away. When the visitor is already a user, he will cancel his account 5% of the time and buy something 15% of the time. If the visitor is a customer, he will cancel his account only 2% of the time and go back to being a user 95% of the time instead of continually buying things.

We could represent the information we have collected in a transition matrix, which shows the probability of going from one state to another, or remaining in the same state (Table 6-1).

Table 6-1. Transition probability

	Prospect	User	Customer
Prospect	0.80	0.15	0.05
User	0.05	0.80	0.15
Customer	0.02	0.95	0.03

What the transition probability defines is known as a *state machine* (see Figure 6-2). It also tells us a lot about how our current customers behave. We can determine the conversion rate, attrition rate, and other probabilities. Conversion rate is the probability of a prospect signing up, which would be 20%—the probability of going from prospect to user plus the probability of prospect to customer (15% + 5%). You could also determine the attrition rate by taking the average of 5% and 2%, which is 3.5%.

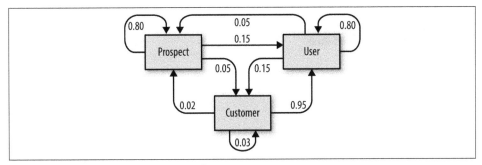

Figure 6-2. User state transition machine

This is an uncommon way of displaying user behavior in analytics, because it is too explanatory. But it has one advantage over traditional conversion rate calculations: the ability to look at how a user operates over time. For instance, we could determine the probability of a user being a prospect given the last four times he was in fact a prospect. This is the probability of being a prospect (say 80%) multiplied by the four times they were a prospect before, which were all 80%. The probability that someone keeps viewing the site and never signs up is low, because eventually he might sign up.

But there is also one major problem with this model: there is no way for us to reliably determine these states without asking each user individually. The state is hidden from our observation. A user can view the site anonymously.

That is actually fine, as you will soon see. As long as we are able to observe interaction with the site and make a judgment call about the underlying transitions from other sources (think Google Analytics), then we can still solve this problem.

We do this by introducing another level of complexity called emissions.

Emissions/Observations of Underlying States

With our preceding example, we don't know when someone goes from being a prospect to a user to a customer. But we are able to observe what a user is doing and what her behavior is. We know that for a given observation there is a probability that she is in a given state.

We can determine the user's underlying state by observing her emitted behaviors. Let's say, for instance, that we have five pages on our website: Home, Signup, Product, Checkout, and Contact Us. Now, as you might imagine, some of these pages matter to us and others do not. For instance, Signup would most likely mean the prospect becomes a user, and Checkout means the user becomes a customer.

This information gets more interesting because we know the probabilities of states. Let's say we know the emission and state probabilities shown in Table 6-2.

Table 6-2. Emission and state probabilities

Page name	Prospect	User	Customer
Home	0.4	0.3	0.3
Signup	0.1	0.8	0.1
Product	0.1	0.3	0.6
Checkout	0	0.1	0.9
Contact Us	0.7	0.1	0.2

We know the probability of users switching states as well as the probability of the behavior they are emitting given the underlying state. Given this info, what is the probability that a user who has viewed the Home, Signup, and Product pages becomes a customer? Namely, we want to solve the problem depicted in Figure 6-3.

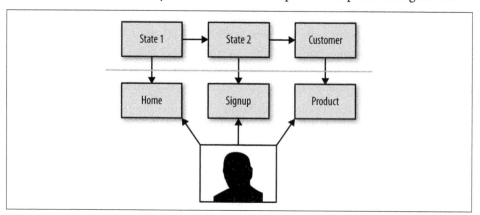

Figure 6-3. States versus observations

To figure this out, we need to determine the probability that a user is in the customer state given all her previous states, or notationally, $P(Customer \mid S_1, S_2)$, as well as the probability of the user viewing the product page given that she was a customer multiplied by the probability of signup given the state, or notationally, $P(Product\_Page \mid Customer)$ * $P(Signup\_Page \mid S_2)$ * $P(Homepage \mid S_1)$. The problem here is that there are more unknowns than knowns.

This finite model is difficult to solve because it involves a lot of calculations. Calculating a problem like $P(Customer \mid S_1, S_2, \cdots, S_N)$ is complicated. To solve this, we need to introduce the Markov assumption.

Emissions and observations are used interchangeably in HMM nomenclature. They are the same thing and refer simply to what a process is emitting or what you can observe.

Simplification Through the Markov Assumption

Remember from the Naive Bayesian Classification that each attribute would independently add to the probability of some events. So for spam, the probability would be independently conditional on words or phrases like *Prince* and *Buy now*. In the model that we're building with user behavior, though, we do want dependence. Mainly, we want the previous state to be part of the next state's probability. In fact, we would assert that the previous states have a relationship to the user's current state.

In the case of Naive Bayesian Classification, we would make the assumption that the probability of something was independently conditional on other events. So spam was independently conditional on each word in the email.

We can do the same with our current system. We can state that the probability of being in a particular state is primarily based on what happened in the previous state. So instead of $P(Customer \mid S_1, S_2, \cdots, S_N)$, our equation would be $P(Customer \mid S_N)$. But why can we get away with such a gross simplification?

Given a state machine like the one we have just defined, the system infers probabilistically and recursively where you have been in the past. For instance, if a site visitor were in the customer state, then you could say that the most probable previous state would be user, and that the most probable state before that would be prospect.

This simplification also has one exciting conclusion, which leads us into our next topic: Markov chains.

Using Markov Chains Instead of a Finite State Machine

We have been talking purely about one system, and only one outcome, thus far. But what is powerful about the Markov assumption is that you can model a system as it operates forever. Instead of looking locally at what the process is going to do, we can figure out how the system will always behave. This brings us to the idea of a Markov chain.

Markov chains are exceptional at simulating systems. Queuing theory, finance, weather modeling, and game theory all make heavy use of Markov chains. They are powerful because they represent behaviors in a concise way. Unlike models such as neural networks, which can become extremely complex as we add nodes, HMMs only rely on a few probability matrices; they are extremely useful at modeling system behaviors.

Markov chains can analyze and find information within an underlying process that will operate forever. But that still doesn't solve our fundamental problem, which is that we still need to determine what state a given person is in given his hidden previous state and our own observations. For that, we will need to enhance Markov chains with a hidden aspect.

Hidden Markov Model

We've talked a lot about observation and underlying state transitions, but now we're almost back to where we started. We still need to figure out what a user's state is. To do this, we will use a Hidden Markov Model, which comprises these three components:

Evaluation
> How likely is it that a sequence like Home → Signup → Product → Checkout will come from our transition and observation of users?

Decoding
> Given this sequence, what does the most likely underlying state sequence look like?

Learning
> Given an observed sequence, what will the user most likely do next?

In the following sections, we will discuss these three elements in detail. First, we'll talk about using the Forward-Backward algorithm to evaluate a sequence of observations. Then we will delve into how to solve the decoding problem with the Viterbi algorithm, which works on a conceptual level. Last, we'll touch on the idea of learning as an extension of decoding.

Evaluation: Forward-Backward Algorithm

Evaluation is a question of figuring out how probable a given sequence is. This is important in determining how likely it is that your model actually created the sequence that you are modeling. It can also be quite useful for determining, for example, if the sequence Home→Home is more probable than Home→Signup. We perform the evaluation step by using the Forward-Backward algorithm. This algorithm's goal is to figure out what the probability of a hidden state is subject to the observations. This is effectively saying that, given some observations, what is the probability that happened?

Mathematical Representation of the Forward-Backward Algorithm

The Forward-Backward algorithm is the probability of an emission happening given its underlying states—that is, $P(e_k \mid s)$. At first glance, this looks difficult because you would have to compute a lot of probabilities to solve it. If we used the chain rule, this could easily become expansive. Fortunately, we can use a simple trick to solve it instead.

The probability of e_k given an observation sequence is proportional to the joint distribution of e_k and the observations:

$$p(e_k \mid s) \propto p(e_k, s)$$

which we can actually split into two separate pieces using the probability chain rule:

$$p(s_{k+1}, s_{k+2}, \cdots, s_n \mid e_k, s_1, s_2, \cdots, s_k) p(e_k, s_1, s_2, \cdots, s_k)$$

This looks fruitless, but we can actually forget about $x_1, \cdots, x_k$ in the first probability because the probabilities are D-Separated. I won't discuss D-Separation too much, but because we're asserting the Markov assumption in our model we can effectively forget about these variables, because they precede what we care about in our probability model:

$$p(e_k \mid s) \propto p(s_{k+1}, s_{k+2}, \cdots, s_n \mid e_k) p(e_k, s_1, s_2, \cdots, s_k)$$

This is the Forward-Backward algorithm!

Graphically, you can imagine this to be a path through this probability space (see Figure 6-4). Given a specific emission at, say, index 2, we could calculate the probability by looking at the forward and backward probabilities.

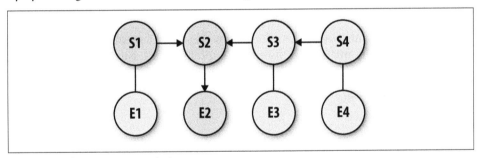

Figure 6-4. States versus emissions

The forward term is looking at the joint probability of the hidden state at point k given all the emissions up to that point. The backward term is looking at the conditional probability of emissions from $k+1$ to the end given that hidden point.

Using User Behavior

Using our preceding example of Home→Signup→Product→Checkout, let's calculate the probability of that sequence happening inside our model using the Forward-Backward algorithm. First let's set up the problem by building a class called Forward Backward:

```
class ForwardBackward:
    def __init__():
```

```
self.observations = ['homepage', 'signup', 'product', 'checkout']
self.states = ['Prospect', 'User', 'Customer']
self.emissions = ['homepage', 'signup', 'product page', 'checkout',\
                  'contact us']

self.start_probability = {
  'Prospect': 0.8,
  'User': 0.15,
  'Customer': 0.05
}

self.transition_probability = np.array([
  [0.8, 0.15, 0.05],
  [0.05, 0.80, 0.15],
  [0.02, 0.95, 0.03]
])

self.emission_probability = np.array([
  [0.4, 0.3, 0.3], # homepage
  [0.1, 0.8, 0.1], # signup
  [0.1, 0.3, 0.6], # product page
  [0, 0.1, 0.9],  # checkout
  [0.7, 0.1, 0.2] # contact us
])

self.end_state = 'Ending'
```

Here we are simply importing the information that we had from before—that is, the transition probability matrix and the emission probabilities. Next, we need to define our foward step, which is:

```
class ForwardBackward:
  # __init__
  def forward():
    forward = []
    f_previous = {}

    for(i in xrange(1, len(self.observations))):
      f_curr = {}
      for(state in self.states):
        if i == 0:
          prev_f_sum = self.start_probability[state]
        else:
          prev_f_sum = 0.0
          for (k in self.states):
            prev_f_sum += f_previous.get(k, 0.0) * \
            self.transition_probability[k][state]
        f_curr[state] = self.emission_probability[state][self.observations[i]]
        f_curr[state] = f_curr[state] * prev_f_sum
        forward.append(f_curr)
        f_previous = f_curr
```

```
    p_fwd = 0.0
    for(k in self.states):
        p_fwd += f_previous[k] * self.transition_probability[k][self.end_state]

    {'probability': p_fwd, 'sequence': forward}
```

The forward algorithm will go through each state at each observation and multiply them together to get a forward probability of how the state works in this given context. Next, we need to define the backward algorithm, which is:

```
class ForwardBackward:
    # __init__
    # forward
    def backward():
        backward = []
        b_prev = {}

        for(i in xrange(len(self.observations), 0, -1)):
            b_curr = {}
            for(state in self.states):
                if i == 0:
                    b_curr[state] = self.transition_probability[state][self.end_state]
                else:
                    sum = 0.0
                    for (k in self.states):
                        sum += self.transition_probability[state][k]* \
                        self.emission_probability[k][self.observations[x_plus]] * \
                        b_prev[k]
            backward.insert(0, b_curr)
            b_prev = b_curr

        p_bkw = 0.0

        for (s in self.states):
            sum += self.start_probability[s] * \
            self.emission_probability[s][self.observations[0]] * \
            b_prev[s]

    {'probability': p_bkw, 'sequence': backward}
```

The backward algorithm works pretty much the same way as the forward one, except that it goes the opposite direction. Next, we need to try both forward and backward and assert that they are the same (otherwise, our algorithm is wrong):

```
class ForwardBackward:
    # __init__
    # forward
    # backward

    def forward_backward():
        size = len(self.observations)
        forward = forward()
        backward = backward()
```

```
posterior = {}
for(s in self.states):
  posterior[s] = []
  for (i in xrange(1, size)):
    value = forward['sequence'][i][s] * \
    backward['sequence'][i][s] / forward['probability'])
  posterior[s].append()

return [forward, backward, posterior]
```

The beauty of the Forward-Backward algorithm is that it's effectively testing itself as it runs. This is quite exciting. It will also solve the problem of evaluation—remember, that means figuring out how probable a given sequence is likely to be. Next, we'll delve into the decoding problem of figuring out the best sequence of underlying states.

The Decoding Problem Through the Viterbi Algorithm

The decoding problem is the easiest to describe. Given a sequence of observations, we want to parse out the best path of states given what we know about them. Mathematically, what we want to find is some specific $\pi^* = \arg\max \pi\ P(x, \pi)$, where π is our state vector and x is the observations.

To achieve this, we use the Viterbi algorithm. You can think of this as a way of constructing a maximum spanning tree. We are trying to figure out, given our current state, what is the best path to approach next. Similar to any sort of greedy algorithm, the Viterbi algorithm just iterates through all possible next steps and takes it.

Graphically, it would look something like Figure 6-5.

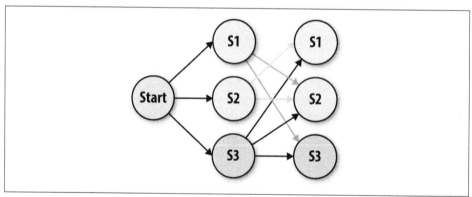

Figure 6-5. Viterbi algorithm

What we see in this figure is how a state like S1 will become less relevant over time, while a state of S3 becomes even more relevant compared to the others. The arrows are shaded to show the probability dampening.

What we are attempting to do with this algorithm is traverse a set of states in the most optimal way. We do this by determining the probability that a state will happen given its emissions as well as the probability that it will transition from the previous state to the current. Then we multiply those two together to get the probability that the sequence will happen. Iterating through the entire sequence, we eventually find our optimal sequence.

The Learning Problem

The learning problem is probably the simplest algorithm to implement. Given a sequence of states and observations, what is the most likely to happen next? We can do that purely by figuring out the next step in the Viterbi sequence. We figure out the next state by maximizing the next step given the fact there is no emission available yet. But you can figure out the most probable emission from there as well as the most probable state, and that is known as the next optimal state emission combo.

If this way of solving doesn't make sense yet, don't worry: in the next section, we will delve further into using the Viterbi algorithm.

Unfortunately, there isn't any free and easily accessible data available for analyzing user behaviors over time given page views, but there is a similar problem we can solve by using a part-of-speech tagger built purely using a Hidden Markov Model.

Part-of-Speech Tagging with the Brown Corpus

Given the phrase "the quick brown fox," how would you tag its parts of speech? We know that English has parts of speech like determiners, adjectives, and nouns. We would probably tag the words in this phrase as determiner, adjective, adjective, noun, respectively. We could fairly easily tag this example because we have a basic understanding of grammar, but how could we train an algorithm to do so?

Well, of course because this is a chapter on HMMs, we'll use one to figure out the optimal parts of speech. Knowing what we know about them, we can use the Viterbi algorithm to figure out, for a given sequence of words, what is the best tagging sequence. For this section, we will rely on the Brown Corpus, which was the first electronic corpus. It has over a million annotated words with parts of speech in it. The list of tags is long, but rest assured that it contains all the normal tags like adjectives, nouns, and verbs.

The Brown Corpus is set up using a specific kind of annotation. For each sequence of words, you will see something like this:

Most/ql important/jj of/in all/abn ,/, the/at less/ql developed/vbn countries/nns must/md be/be persuaded/vbn to/to take/vb the/at necessary/jj steps/nns to/to allocate/vb and/cc commit/vb their/pp$ own/jj resources/nns ./.

In this case, *Most* is *ql*, which means qualifier, *important* is *jj* (adjective), and so on until you reach ./. which is a period tagged as a stop: " . ".

The only thing that this doesn't have is a START character at the beginning. Generally speaking, when we're writing Markov models, we want the word at t and also the word at t – 1. Because *most* is at the front, there is no word before it, so therefore we just use a special name, START, to show that there is a start to this sequence. That way we can measure the probability of going from START to a qualifier.

Setup Notes

All of the code we're using for this example can be found on GitHub (*https://github.com/thoughtfulml/examples-in-python/tree/master/hidden_markov_model*).

Python is constantly changing, so the README file is the best place to find out how to run the examples.

There are no other dependencies for getting this example to run with Python.

Coding and Testing Design

The overall approach we will be taking to write our part-of-speech tagger is to have two classes (Figure 6-6):

CorpusParser
    This class is responsible for parsing the Brown Corpus.

POSTagger
    This class is responsible for tagging new data given the corpus training data.

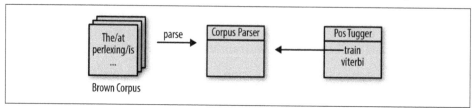

Figure 6-6. Class diagram for part-of-speech tagger

Our tests in this case will focus on writing good seam tests around the Brown Corpus and cross-validating an error rate that is acceptable.

The Seam of Our Part-of-Speech Tagger: CorpusParser

The *seam* of a part-of-speech tagger is how you feed it data. The most important point is to feed it proper information so the part-of-speech tagger can utilize and learn from that data. First we need to make some assumptions about how we want it to work. We want to store each transition from a word tag combo in an array of two and then wrap that array in a simple class called CorpusParser::TagWord. Our initial test looks like this:

```python
import unittest

from hidden_markov_model.corpus_parser import CorpusParser

class TestCorpusParser(unittest.TestCase):
  def setUp(self):
    self.stream = '\tSeveral/ap defendants/nns ./.\n'
    self.blank = '\t    \n'

  def test_parse(self):
    """will parse a brown corpus line using the standard / notation"""
    cp = CorpusParser()

    null = CorpusParser.TagWord('START', 'START')
    several = CorpusParser.TagWord('Several', 'ap')
    defendants = CorpusParser.TagWord('defendants', 'nns')
    period = CorpusParser.TagWord('.', '.')

    expectations = [
      [null, several],
      [several, defendants],
      [defendants, period]
    ]

    results = list(cp.parse(self.stream))
    self.assertListEqual(expectations, results)

  def test_blank(self):
    """does not allow blank lines from happening"""
    cp = CorpusParser()

    results = list(cp.parse(self.blank))
    self.assertEqual(0, len(results))
```

This code takes two cases that are Brown Corpus–like and checks to make sure they are being parsed properly. The first case is whether we can parse stream correctly into tokens. The second case is a gut check to make sure it ignores blank lines, as the Brown Corpus is full of them.

Filling in the CorpusParser class, we would have something that initially looks like this:

```python
import collections
from copy import copy


class CorpusParser:
    """
    This class is responsible for parsing the Brown Corpus.
    """
    NULL_CHARACTER = 'START'
    STOP = ' \n'
    SPLITTER = '/'

    def __init__(self):
        self.ngram = 2

    TagWord = collections.namedtuple('TagWord', ['word', 'tag'])

    def parse(self, stream):
        """
        Parse Brown Corps
        :param stream: string of text
        :return: an iterator through ngraps
        """
        ngrams = self.ngram * [CorpusParser.TagWord(CorpusParser.NULL_CHARACTER,
                                                     CorpusParser.NULL_CHARACTER)]
        word = ''
        pos = ''
        parse_word = True

        for char in stream:
            if char == '\t' or (len(word) == 0 and char in CorpusParser.STOP):
                continue
            elif char == CorpusParser.SPLITTER:
                parse_word = False
            elif char in CorpusParser.STOP:
                ngrams.pop(0)
                ngrams.append(CorpusParser.TagWord(word, pos))

                yield copy(ngrams)

                word = ''
                pos = ''
                parse_word = True
            elif parse_word:
                word += char
            else:
                pos += char

        if len(word) > 0 and len(pos) > 0:
            ngrams.pop(0)
            ngrams.append(CorpusParser.TagWord(word, pos))
            yield copy(ngrams)
```

As in the previous chapters, implementing a parser using each_char is generally the most performant way of parsing things in Python. Now we can get into the much more interesting part: writing the part-of-speech tagger.

Writing the Part-of-Speech Tagger

At this point we are ready to write our part-of-speech tagger class. To do this we will have to take care of the following:

1. Take data from the CorpusParser
2. Store it internally so we can calculate the probabilities of word tag combos
3. Do the same for tag transitions

We want this class to be able to tell us how probable a word and tag sequence is, and to determine from a plaintext sentence what the optimal tag sequence is.

To be able to do that, we need to tackle calculating probabilities first, then calculate the probability of a tag sequence with a word sequence. Last, we'll implement the Viterbi algorithm.

Let's talk about the probability of a tag given its previous tag. Using something called a maximum likelihood estimate, we can assert that the probability should equal the count of the two tags together divided by the count of the previous tag. A test for that would look like this:

```python
import unittest

from io import StringIO
from hidden_markov_model.pos_tagger import POSTagger

class TestProbabilityCalculation(unittest.TestCase):
    def setUp(self):
        self.stream = u'A/B C/D C/D A/D A/B ./.'
        self.pos_tagger = POSTagger([StringIO(self.stream)])
        self.pos_tagger.train()

    def test_calculate_tag_transition_probabilities(self):
        self.assertAlmostEqual(0, self.pos_tagger.tag_probability('Z', 'Z'))
        self.assertAlmostEqual(2.0 / 3, self.pos_tagger.tag_probability('D', 'D'))
        self.assertAlmostEqual(1, self.pos_tagger.tag_probability('START', 'B'))
        self.assertAlmostEqual(0.5, self.pos_tagger.tag_probability('B', 'D'))
        self.assertAlmostEqual(0, self.pos_tagger.tag_probability('.', 'D'))
```

Which we can make pass by the following code.

```python
from collections import defaultdict
import re

from hidden_markov_model.corpus_parser import CorpusParser
```

```python
class POSTagger(object):
    """
    This class is responsible for tagging new data given the corpus training data.
    """

    def __init__(self, data_io=(), eager=False):
        self.corpus_parser = CorpusParser()
        self.data_io = data_io
        self.trained = False
        if eager:
            self.train()
            self.trained = True

    def train(self):
        if not self.trained:
            self.tags = set()
            self.tag_combos = defaultdict(int)
            self.tag_frequencies = defaultdict(int)
            self.word_tag_combos = defaultdict(int)

            for io in self.data_io:
                for line in io:
                    for ngram in self.corpus_parser.parse(line):
                        self.write(ngram)
            self.trained = True

    def write(self, ngram):
        """
        :param ngram:
        """
        if ngram[0].tag == 'START':
            self.tag_frequencies['START'] += 1
            self.word_tag_combos['START/START'] += 1

        self.tags.add(ngram[-1].tag)

        self.tag_frequencies[ngram[-1].tag] += 1
        combo = ngram[-1].word + '/' + ngram[-1].tag
        self.word_tag_combos[combo] += 1
        combo = ngram[0].tag + '/' + ngram[-1].tag
        self.tag_combos[combo] += 1

    def tag_probability(self, previous_tag, current_tag):
        """Maximum likelihood estimate
        count(previous_tag, current_tag) / count(previous_tag)"""
        denom = self.tag_frequencies[previous_tag]

        if denom == 0:
            return 0
        else:
            return self.tag_combos[previous_tag + '/' + current_tag] / float(denom)
```

Remember that the sequence starts with an implied tag called START. So here you see the probability of D transitioning to D is in fact two divided by three, because D transitions to D two times but D shows up three times in that sequence.

Default Dictionaries

Dictionaries in Python are similar to associative arrays, hashes, or hashmaps. The general concept is the same: store some sort of key value pair in a data structure. Default dictionaries, on the other hand, take it a bit further. In most cases when defining a dictionary in Python, if you ask for something that isn't in the dictionary you would get a KeyError.

Instead, with default dictionaries you can set a default to always return.

```
from collections import defaultdict

dictionary = {'a': 'b'}
dictionary['b'] # Yields KeyError

default_dictionary = defaultdict(lambda: 0, dictionary)
default_dictionary['b'] == 0
```

You'll notice that we're doing a bit of error handling for the case when zeros happen, because we will throw a divide-by-zero error. Next, we need to address the probability of word tag combinations, which we can do by introducing the following to our existing test:

```
class TestProbabilityCalculation(unittest.TestCase):
  # setUp
  # test_calculate_tag_transition_probabilities

  def test_probability_of_word_tag(self):
    """calculates the probability of a word given a tag"""
    self.assertAlmostEqual(0, self.pos_tagger.word_tag_probability('Z', 'Z'))
    self.assertAlmostEqual(1, self.pos_tagger.word_tag_probability('A', 'B'))
    self.assertAlmostEqual(1.0 / 3, self.pos_tagger.word_tag_probability('A', 'D'))
    self.assertAlmostEqual(1, self.pos_tagger.word_tag_probability('.', '.'))
```

To make this work in the POSTagger class, we need to write the following:

```
class POSTagger(object):
  # __init__
  # train
  # write
  # tag_probability

  def word_tag_probability(self, word, tag):
    """Maximum Likelihood estimate
    count (word and tag) / count(tag)"""
```

```
        denom = self.tag_frequencies[tag]
        if denom == 0:
            return 0
        else:
            return self.word_tag_combos[word + '/' + tag] / float(denom)
```

Now that we have those two things—word_tag_probability and tag_probability —we can answer the question: given a word and tag sequence, how probable is it? That is the probability of the current tag given the previous tag, multiplied by the word given the tag. In a test, it looks like this:

```
class TestProbabilityCalculation(unittest.TestCase):
    # setUp
    # test_calculate_tag_transition_probabilities
    # test_probability_of_word_tag

    def test_calculate_words_and_tags(self):
        """calculates probability of sequence of words and tags"""
        words = ['START', 'A', 'C', 'A', 'A', '.']
        tags = ['START', 'B', 'D', 'D', 'B', '.']
        tag_probabilities = self.pos_tagger.tag_probability('B', 'D') * \
                            self.pos_tagger.tag_probability('D', 'D') * \
                            self.pos_tagger.tag_probability('D', 'B') * \
                            self.pos_tagger.tag_probability('B', '.')
        word_probabilities = self.pos_tagger.word_tag_probability('A', 'B') * \
                             self.pos_tagger.word_tag_probability('C', 'D') * \
                             self.pos_tagger.word_tag_probability('A', 'D') * \
                             self.pos_tagger.word_tag_probability('A', 'B')
        expected = word_probabilities * tag_probabilities
        result = self.pos_tagger.probability_of_word_tag(words, tags)
        self.assertAlmostEqual(expected, result)
```

So basically we are calculating word tag probabilities multiplied by the probability of tag transitions. We can easily implement this in the POSTagger class using the following:

```
class POSTagger(object):
    # __init__
    # train
    # write
    # tag_probability
    # word_tag_probability

    def probability_of_word_tag(self, words, tags):
        if len(words) != len(tags):
            raise ValueError('The word and tags must be the same length!')

        length = len(words)

        probability = 1.0

        for i in range(1, length):
```

```
        probability *= self.tag_probability(tags[i - 1], tags[i]) * \
                        self.word_tag_probability(words[i], tags[i])

    return probability
```

Now we can figure out how probable a given word and tag sequence is. But it would be better if we were able to determine, given a sentence and training data, what the optimal sequence of tags is. For that, we need to write this simple test:

```
import unittest

from io import StringIO
from hidden_markov_model.pos_tagger import POSTagger


class TestViterbi(unittest.TestCase):
  def setUp(self):
    self.training = u'I/PRO want/V to/TO race/V ./. I/PRO like/V cats/N ./.'
    self.sentence = 'I want to race.'
    self.pos_tagger = POSTagger([StringIO(self.training)])
    self.pos_tagger.train()

  def test(self):
    """will calculate the best viterbi sequence for I want to race"""
    expectation = ['START', 'PRO', 'V', 'TO', 'V', '.']
    result = self.pos_tagger.viterbi(self.sentence)
    self.assertListEqual(expectation, result)
```

This test takes a bit more to implement because the Viterbi algorithm is somewhat involved. So let's go through this step by step. The first problem is that our method accepts a string, not a sequence of tokens. We need to split by whitespace and treat stop characters as their own word. So to do that, we write the following to set up the Viterbi algorithm:

```
class POSTagger(object):
  #__init__
  # train
  # write
  # tag_probability
  # word_tag_probability
  # probability_of_word_tag

  def viterbi(self, sentence):
    sentence1 = re.sub(r'([\.\?!])', r' \1', sentence)
    parts = re.split(r'\s+', sentence1)
```

The Viterbi algorithm is an iterative algorithm, meaning at each step it figures out where it should go next based on the previous answer. So we will need to memoize the previous probabilities as well as keep the best tag. We can initialize and figure out what the best tag is as follows:

```
class POSTagger(object):
  #__init__
  # train
  # write
  # tag_probability
  # word_tag_probability
  # probability_of_word_tag

  def viterbi(sentence):
    # parts
    last_viterbi = {}
    backpointers = ['START']

    for tag in self.tags:
      if tag == 'START':
        continue
      else:
        probability = self.tag_probability('START', tag) \
                      * self.word_tag_probability(parts[0], tag)

        if probability > 0:
          last_viterbi[tag] = probability
    if len(last_viterbi) > 0:
      backpointer = max(last_viterbi,
                        key=(lambda key: last_viterbi[key]))
    else:
      backpointer = max(self.tag_frequencies,
                        key=(lambda key: self.tag_frequencies[key]))
    backpointers.append(backpointer)
```

At this point, last_viterbi has only one option, which is {*PRO*: 1.0}. That is because the probability of transitioning from START to anything else is zero. Likewise, back pointers will have START and PRO in it. So, now that we've set up our initial step, all we need to do is iterate through the rest:

```
class POSTagger(object):
  #__init__
  # train
  # write
  # tag_probability
  # word_tag_probability
  # probability_of_word_tag

  def viterbi(sentence):
    # parts
    # initialization
    for part in parts[1:]:
      viterbi = {}
      for tag in self.tags:
        if tag == 'START':
          continue
        if len(last_viterbi) == 0:
```

```
                break

        best_tag = max(last_viterbi,
                       key=(lambda prev_tag: last_viterbi[prev_tag] *
                                 self.tag_probability(prev_tag, tag) *
                                 self.word_tag_probability(part, tag)))

        probability = last_viterbi[best_tag] * \
                 self.tag_probability(best_tag, tag) * \
                 self.word_tag_probability(part, tag)

        if probability > 0:
          viterbi[tag] = probability

    last_viterbi = viterbi

    if len(last_viterbi) > 0:
      backpointer = max(last_viterbi,
                        key=(lambda key: last_viterbi[key]))
    else:
      backpointer = max(self.tag_frequencies,
                        key=(lambda key: self.tag_frequencies[key]))
    backpointers.append(backpointer)

  return backpointers
```

What we are doing is storing only relevant information, and if there's a case where `last_viterbi` is empty, we'll use `tag_frequencies` instead. That case really only happens when we have pruned too far. But this approach is much faster than storing all of the information in memory.

At this point, things should work! But how well?

Cross-Validating to Get Confidence in the Model

At this stage, it is prudent to write a cross-validation test. This is using a naive model, but we want to see at least 20% accuracy. So let's write this into a tenfold cross-validation spec. Instead of requiring that this model be within a range of confidence, we will just display the error rate to the user. When I ran the test on my machine, I got around a 30% error rate. We will talk about how to improve this, but for our purposes, it's good given that it looks at only two probabilities:

```
import glob
import unittest

import re
from hidden_markov_model.pos_tagger import POSTagger

class TestCrossValidation(unittest.TestCase):
  FOLDS = 10
```

```
def setUp(self):
  self.files = glob.glob('data/brown/c???')

def test(self):
  for i in range(TestCrossValidation.FOLDS):
    print("test cross validation for fold %d" % i)
    splits = int(len(self.files) / TestCrossValidation.FOLDS)
    validation_indexes = range(i * splits, (i + 1) * splits)

    training_indexes = list(set(range(len(self.files))).
                            difference(validation_indexes))
    validation_files = [fn for idx, fn in enumerate(self.files)
                        if idx in validation_indexes]
    training_files = [fn for idx, fn in enumerate(self.files)
                      if idx in training_indexes]

    pos_tagger = POSTagger.from_filepaths(training_files, True)

    misses = 0
    successes = 0

    for vf in validation_files:
      with open(vf, 'r') as f:
        for l in f:
          if re.match(r'\A\s+\Z', l):
            continue
          words = []
          parts_of_speech = ['START']
          for ppp in re.split(r'\s+', l.strip()):
            z = ppp.split('/')
            words.append(z[0])
            parts_of_speech.append(z[1])

          tag_seq = pos_tagger.viterbi(' '.join(words))
          for tag1, tag2 in zip(tag_seq, parts_of_speech):
            if tag1 == tag2:
              successes += 1
            else:
              misses += 1
    print(misses / float(misses + successes))
    print('Error rate was %f' % (misses / float(misses + successes)))
```

This will yield around a 20% to 30% error rate, which realistically isn't accurate. Part of the problem, though, is that the Brown Corpus makes a lot of distinctions between tags, so the error rate would be much lower if you didn't care about, say, possessive pronouns versus regular pronouns.

How to Make This Model Better

As with all of our coding examples, the best way to improve this model is to first determine how well it works and to iterate. One quick way to make this model operate better would be to look back more than one word at a time. So instead of the probability of a tag given the previous tag, you'd find the probability of a tag given the previous two tags. You could do that by modifying the corpus tagger. But the example does work well and is simple to make!

While it seems pedestrian to model part of speech tagging, what we've shown here actually could be used to build a user state model, which we talked about earlier. While I don't have access to that kind of data I can distribute freely, this could be used to look at observations of log data and then mark users as being of a given state (customer, user, prospect).

Taking this even further, we could use this model as a generative process to build intuition around how our users behave, and when they become less engaged.

Conclusion

Hidden Markov models are some of the most interesting models when it comes to determining underlying data from a system given some observable data. For example, you can determine the real state of a user, find the underlying tag of a word, or even follow musical scores.

In this chapter, you learned about how state machines can be generalized into Markov chains, which then can be used to model system behavior forever. We also added a hidden component to determine the underlying state of a model given emissions that we can easily observe. You learned that the three stages of using HMMs are evaluation, decoding, and learning, and how to approach solving those problems. Last, we tagged parts of speech using the Brown Corpus and the Viterbi algorithm.

## CHAPTER 7

Support Vector Machines

In this chapter, we will set out to solve a common problem: determining whether customers are happy or not. We'll approach this by understanding that happy customers generally say nice things while unhappy ones don't. This is their sentiment.

There are an infinite amount of solutions to this problem, but this chapter will focus on just one that works well: support vector machines (SVMs). This algorithm uses decision boundaries to split data into multiple parts and operates well in higher dimensions due to feature transformation and ignoring distances between data points. We will discuss the normal testing methods we have laid out before, such as:

- Cross-validation
- Confusion matrix
- Precision and recall

But we will also delve into a new way of improving models, known as *feature transformation*. In addition, we will discuss the possibilities of the following phenomena happening in a problem of sentiment analysis:

- Entanglement
- Unstable data
- Correction cascade
- Configuration debt

Customer Happiness as a Function of What They Say

Our online store has two sets of customers, happy and unhappy. The happy customers return to the site consistently and buy from the company, while the unhappy customers are either window shoppers or spendthrifts who don't care about the company or who are spending their money elsewhere. Our goals are to determine whether customer happiness correlates with our bottom line, and, down the line, to monitor their happiness.

But here exists a problem. How do we numerically say that a customer is happy or not? Unfortunately, there isn't a field in our database explaining how happy our customers are. We know intuitively that happy customers are usually more likely to stay customers, but how can we *test* that?

There are two tiers to this problem:

1. We need to figure out whether customers are happy or not, or whether their sentiment is positive or negative in what they say.

2. Does overall customer sentiment correlate with our bottom line?

We also assume that a happy customer means more money, but is that actually true? How can we even build an algorithm to test something like that?

To start solving this two-tiered problem, we will figure a way to map customers to sentiment. There are many ways to approach this problem such as clustering customers into two groups or using KNN to find the closest neighbors to people we *know* are *unhappy* or *happy*. Or we could use SVMs.

Sentiment Classification Using SVMs

To be able to map overall customer sentiment, we first need data to use. For our purposes we have a support system that allows us to export data that was written by our customers.

Thinking about our customers who have written to us many times in our support system, how would we determine whether they are happy or not? Ways to approach this include:

- Have support agents tag each individual ticket with a sentiment (positive or negative).

- Have support agents tag a subset of tickets (X% of all tickets).

- Use an existing tagged database (such as movie reviews or some academic data set).

Data Collection

Even though in this chapter we will use an academic data set for the example, I do want to point out that having a group of people tag a subset is generally the right way to approach this problem.

In practice we want to achieve the best results for the least amount of work—that is, getting a good set of *ground truth* around a problem. In the case of sentiment analysis, if we were to do this as a product for a company, most likely we would have support agents collect a subset of tickets (say 30% of all tickets) and as a group tag them either negative or positive.

An important point here, though, is that humans differ on problems like this. Person A might think a ticket is positive, while Person B thinks the ticket is negative.

For this reason, it's important to apply some sort of voting mechanism, whether it's a mean or mode. So if we were to tag 30% of all tickets we would want at least three people tagging each ticket so we could either average the answers or find the most common answer.

This can actually be used to bootstrap a data set as well. Generally the more consensus there is on a data point, the more likely a machine learning algorithm will be able to classify it.

Now that we have data to classify, we can determine what algorithm to use. Since this chapter is about using SVMs, we are going to use that, although many other algorithms would work just as well. I've decided to use SVMs in this chapter, though, because they have the following properties:

- They avoid the curse of dimensionality, meaning we can use lots of dimensions (features).
- They have been shown to work well with sentiment analysis, which is pertinent to the issues discussed next.[1]

The Theory Behind SVMs

Let's imagine we have data from our customers, in this case support tickets. In this example let's say the customer is either happy or unhappy with the ticket (Figure 7-1).

---

[1] Gaurangi Patil et al., "Sentiment Analysis Using Support Vector Machine," *International Journal of Innovative Research in Computer and Communication Engineering* 2, no. 1 (2014), *http://ijircce.com/upload/2014/january/16K_Sentiment.pdf*.

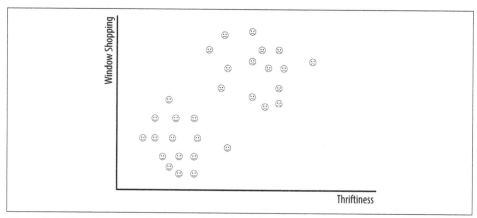

Figure 7-1. Happiness as a function of window shopping and thriftiness

Conceptually, if we were to build a model of what makes a customer happy or unhappy, we could take our inputs (in this case features from the text) and determine customer groupings. This would be very similar to KNN and would yield something like Figure 7-2.

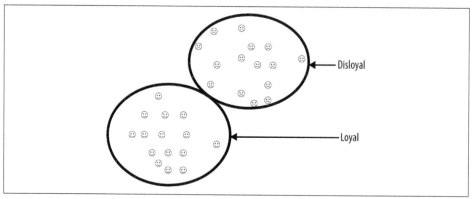

Figure 7-2. Loyal and disloyal customers

This is a great idea, but it has a downside: textual features generally are high in number, which as we've discussed can incur the *curse of dimensionality*. For instance, given a set of support tickets there might be 4,000 dimensions, each defining whether they said a word in a corpus. So instead of relying on KNN, we should approach this model via a decision boundary.

Decision Boundary

If you were to look at these data points as a graphic, you might also think about splitting the data into two pieces by drawing a line down the middle. It's obvious to us humans that this might yield a good solution. It also means that anything on one side of the line is unhappy while anything on the other is happy.

This idea is called a *decision boundary method* and there are many different algorithms in this category, including rules-based algorithms and decision trees.

Decision trees and random forests are types of decision boundary methods. If we were to plot the mushrooms on a n-dimensional plane, we could construct a boundary that splits the data into its various points.

But for sentiment analysis with 4,000 dimensions, given what we see here, how can we find the best boundary that splits the data into two parts?

Maximizing Boundaries

To find the most optimal line between the two sets of data, imagine that we instead draw a margin between the two data pieces (Figure 7-3). If you could find the widest margin between the two data sets, then you would have solved the problem optimally and also found the solution that SVMs find.

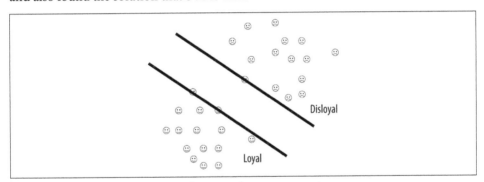

Figure 7-3. Maximize the margin between the two categories

This is what SVMs do: maximize the breadth of the margin between two (or more) classifications. The beauty of this algorithm is that it is computationally optimal because it maps to a quadratic program (a convex optimization).

But as you might notice I'm cheating by showing data that can be separated by a line. What about data where things aren't so pretty?

Kernel Trick: Feature Transformation

What if our data isn't linear? This is where a fundamental concept of improving and testing models comes into play. Instead of being forced to live in a coordinate system such as $<x_0, \cdots, x_1>$, we can instead transform our data into a new coordinate system that is easier to solve. There are lots of ways of transforming features (which we will cover in later chapters) but one of them is called the kernel trick.

To understand it, here's a riddle for you: in Figure 7-4, draw a straight line that separates the two circles.

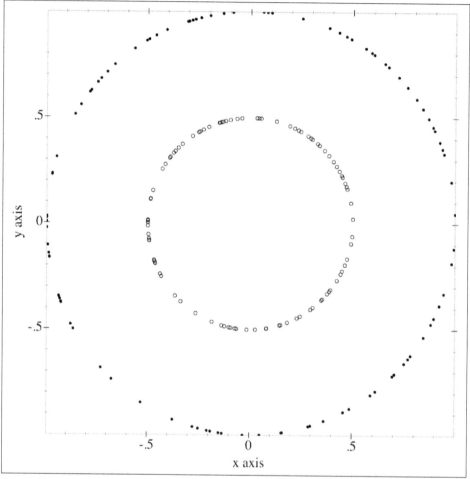

Figure 7-4. Two circles inside of each other can't be separated by drawing a straight line

Well, you can't. That is, unless you think outside of the box, so to speak.

These look like regular circles, so there doesn't appear to be a line that you could separate them with. This is true in 2D Cartesian coordinate systems, but if you project this into a 3D Cartesian coordinate system, $< x,y > \rightarrow <x^2,\sqrt{2}xy,y^2>$, you will find that in fact this turns out to be linear (Figure 7-5).

Now you can see that these two circles are separate and you can draw a plane easily between the two. If you took that and mapped it back to the original plane, then there would in fact be a third circle in the middle that is a straight plane.

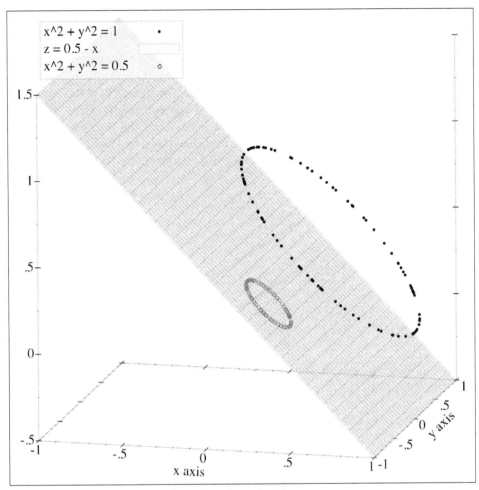

Figure 7-5. Separating two circles using a kernel trick

Next time you need a bar trick, try that out on someone.

This doesn't just work for circles, but unfortunately the visualizations of four or more dimensions are confusing so I left them out. There are many different types of projections (or kernels) such as:

- Polynomial kernel (heterogeneous and homogeneous)
- Radial basis functions
- Gaussian kernels

I do encourage you to read up more on kernels, although they will most likely distract us from the original intent of this section!

One downside to using kernels, though, is that you can easily overfit data. In a lot of ways they operate like splines. But one way to avoid overfitting is to introduce slack.

Optimizing with Slack

What if our data isn't separable by a line? Luckily mathematicians have thought about this, and in mathematical optimization there's a concept called "slack." This idea introduces another variable that is minimized but reduces the worry of overfit. In practice, with SVMs the amount of slack is determined by a free parameter C, which could be thought of as a way to tell the algorithm how much slack to add or not (Figure 7-6).

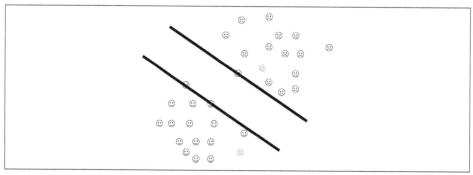

Figure 7-6. Slack introduced into model. The highlighted faces are basically wrong or incorrect data points.

As I discussed in Chapter 5, overfitting is a downfall of machine learning and inductive biases, so avoiding it is a good thing to do.

Okay, enough theory—let's build a sentiment analyzer.

Sentiment Analyzer

In this section, we'll build a sentiment analyzer that determines the sentiment of movie reviews. The example we'll use also applies to working with support tickets. We'll first talk about what this tool will look like conceptually in a class diagram. Then, after identifying the pieces of the tool, we will build a Corpus class, a CorpusSet class, and a SentimentClassifier class. The Corpus and CorpusSet classes involve transforming the text into numerical information. SentimentClassifier is where we will then use the SVM algorithm to build this sentiment analyzer.

Setup Notes

All of the code we are using for this example can be found on the *thoughtfulml* repository on GitHub (*https://github.com/thoughtfulml/examples-in-python/tree/master/support_vector_machines*).

Python is constantly changing, so the README file is the best place to get up to speed on running the examples.

There are no additional dependencies beyond a running Python version to run this example.

Coding and Testing Design

In this section we will be building three classes to support classifying incoming text to either positive or negative sentiment (Figure 7-7).

Corpus
> This class will parse sentiment text and store as a corpus with frequencies in it.

CorpusSet
> This is a collection of multiple corpora that each have a sentiment attached to it.

SentimentClassifier
> Utilizes a CorpusSet to train and classify sentiment.

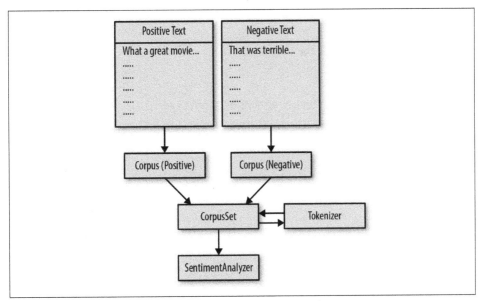

Figure 7-7. Class diagram for movie-review sentiment analyzer

What Do Corpus and Corpora Mean?

Corpus, like corpse, means a body, but in this case it's a body of writings. This word is used heavily in the natural-language processing community to signal a big group of previous writings that can be used to infer knowledge. In our example, we are using *corpus* to refer to a body of writings around a certain sentiment. *Corpora* is the plural of *corpus*.

Testing in SVMs primarily deals with setting a threshold of acceptance with accuracy and then tweaking the model until it works well enough. That is the concept we will apply in this chapter.

SVM Testing Strategies

Besides the normal TDD affair of writing unit tests for our seams and building a solid code basis, there are additional testing considerations for SVMs:

- Speed of training the model before and after configuration changes
- Confusion matrix and precision and recall
- Sensitivity analysis (correction cascades, configuration debt)

I will talk about these concerns through this section.

Corpus Class

Our Corpus class will handle the following:

- Tokenizing text
- Sentiment leaning, whether :negative or :positive
- Mapping from sentiment leaning to a numerical value
- Returning a unique set of words from the corpus

When we write the seam test for this, we end up with the following:

```
import unittest

from io import StringIO
from support_vector_machines.corpus import Corpus

class TestCorpusSet(unittest.TestCase):
  def setUp(self):
    self.negative = StringIO('I hated that so much')
    self.negative_corpus = Corpus(self.negative, 'negative')
    self.positive = StringIO('loved movie!! loved')
    self.positive_corpus = Corpus(self.positive, 'positive')
```

```
def test_trivial(self):
    """consumes multiple files and turns it into sparse vectors"""
    self.assertEqual('negative', self.negative_corpus.sentiment)

def test_tokenize1(self):
    """downcases all the word tokens"""
    self.assertListEqual(['quick', 'brown', 'fox'],
                         Corpus.tokenize('Quick Brown Fox'))

def test_tokenize2(self):
    """ignores all stop symbols"""
    self.assertListEqual(['hello'], Corpus.tokenize('"\'hello!?!?!.\'"  '))

def test_tokenize3(self):
    """ignores the unicode space"""
    self.assertListEqual(['hello', 'bob'], Corpus.tokenize(u'hello\u00A0bob'))

def test_positive(self):
    """consumes a positive training set"""
    self.assertEqual('positive', self.positive_corpus.sentiment)

def test_words(self):
    """consumes a positive training set and unique set of words"""
    self.assertEqual({'loved', 'movie'}, self.positive_corpus.get_words())

def test_sentiment_code_1(self):
    """defines a sentiment_code of 1 for positive"""
    self.assertEqual(1, Corpus(StringIO(''), 'positive').sentiment_code)

def test_sentiment_code_minus1(self):
    """defines a sentiment_code of 1 for positive"""
    self.assertEqual(-1, Corpus(StringIO(''), 'negative').sentiment_code)
```

 StringIO makes strings look like IO objects, which makes it easy to
test file IO–type operations on strings.

As you learned in Chapter 4, there are many different ways of tokenizing text, such as
extracting out stems, frequency of letters, emoticons, and words. For our purposes,
we will just tokenize words. These are defined as strings between nonalpha characters. So out of a string like "The quick brown fox" we would extract *the*, *quick*, *brown*,
fox (Figure 7-8). We don't care about punctuation and we want to be able to skip Unicode spaces and nonwords.

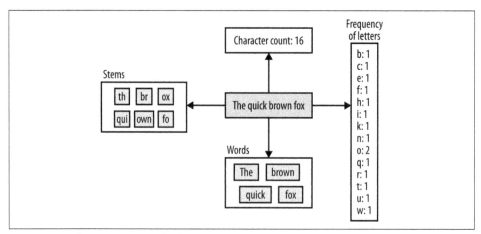

Figure 7-8. The many ways of tokenizing text

Writing the Corpus class, we end up with:

```python
import io
import re


class Corpus(object):
  skip_regex = re.compile(r'[\'"\.\?\!]+')
  space_regex = re.compile(r'\s', re.UNICODE)
  stop_words = [x.strip() \
                for x in io.open('data/stopwords.txt', errors='ignore').readlines()]
  sentiment_to_number = {'positive': 1, 'negative': -1}

  @classmethod
  def tokenize(cls, text):
    cleared_text = cls.skip_regex.sub('', text)
    parts = cls.space_regex.split(cleared_text)
    parts = [part.lower() for part in parts]
    return [part for part in parts if len(part) > 0 and part not in cls.stop_words]

  def __init__(self, io, sentiment):
    self._io = io
    self._sentiment = sentiment
    self._words = None

  @property
  def sentiment(self):
    return self._sentiment

  @property
  def sentiment_code(self):
    return self.sentiment_to_number[self._sentiment]

  def get_words(self):
```

```
      if self._words is None:
        self._words = set()
        for line in self._io:
          for word in Corpus.tokenize(line):
            self._words.add(word)
        self._io.seek(0)
      return self._words

    def get_sentences(self):
      for line in self._io:
        yield line
```

Now to create our next class, CorpusSet.

CorpusSet Class

The CorpusSet class brings multiple corpora together and gives us a good basis to use SVMs:

```
import unittest

from io import StringIO
from numpy import array
from scipy.sparse import csr_matrix
from support_vector_machines.corpus import Corpus
from support_vector_machines.corpus_set import CorpusSet


class TestCorpusSet(unittest.TestCase):
  def setUp(self):
    self.positive = StringIO('I love this country')
    self.negative = StringIO('I hate this man')

    self.positive_corp = Corpus(self.positive, 'positive')
    self.negative_corp = Corpus(self.negative, 'negative')

    self.corpus_set = CorpusSet([self.positive_corp, self.negative_corp])

  def test_compose(self):
    """composes two corpuses together"""
    self.assertEqual({'love', 'country', 'hate', 'man'},
                     self.corpus_set.words)

  def test_spars(self):
    """returns a set of sparse vectors to train on"""
    expected_ys = [1, -1]
    expected_xes = csr_matrix(array(
      [[1, 1, 0, 0],
       [0, 0, 1, 1]]
    ))

    self.corpus_set.calculate_sparse_vectors()
```

```
    ys = self.corpus_set.yes
    xes = self.corpus_set.xes

    self.assertListEqual(expected_ys, ys)
    self.assertListEqual(list(expected_xes.data),
                         list(xes.data))
    self.assertListEqual(list(expected_xes.indices),
                         list(xes.indices))
    self.assertListEqual(list(expected_xes.indptr),
                         list(xes.indptr))
```

To make these tests pass, we need to build a CorpusSet class that takes in multiple corpora, transforms all of that into a matrix of features, and has the properties words, xes, and yes (the latter for x's and y's).

Let's start by building a CorpusSet class:

```
import numpy as np
from scipy.sparse import csr_matrix, vstack

from .corpus import Corpus


class CorpusSet(object):
  def __init__(self, corpora):
    self._yes = None
    self._xes = None
    self._corpora = corpora
    self._words = set()
    for corpus in self._corpora:
      self._words.update(corpus.get_words())

  @property
  def words(self):
    return self._words

  @property
  def xes(self):
    return self._xes

  @property
  def yes(self):
    return self._yes
```

This doesn't do much except store all of the words in a set for later use. It does that by iterating the corpora and storing all the unique words. From here we need to calculate the sparse vectors we will use in the SVM, which depends on building a feature matrix composed of feature vectors:

```
class CorpusSet(object):
  # __init__
  # words
```

```
# xes
# yes
def calculate_sparse_vectors(self):
  self._yes = []
  self._xes = None
  for corpus in self._corpora:
    vectors = self.feature_matrix(corpus)
    if self._xes is None:
      self._xes = vectors
    else:
      self._xes = vstack((self._xes, vectors))
    self._yes.extend([corpus.sentiment_code] * vectors.shape[0])

def feature_matrix(self, corpus):
  data = []
  indices = []
  indptr = [0]
  for sentence in corpus.get_sentences():
    sentence_indices = self._get_indices(sentence)
    indices.extend(sentence_indices)
    data.extend([1] * len(sentence_indices))
    indptr.append(len(indices))
  feature_matrix = csr_matrix((data, indices, indptr),
                              shape=(len(indptr) - 1,
                                     len(self._words)),
                              dtype=np.float64)
  feature_matrix.sort_indices()
  return feature_matrix

def feature_vector(self, sentence):
  indices = self._get_indices(sentence)
  data = [1] * len(indices)
  indptr = [0, len(indices)]
  vector = csr_matrix((data, indices, indptr),
                      shape=(1, len(self._words)),
                      dtype=np.float64)
  return vector

def _get_indices(self, sentence):
  word_list = list(self._words)
  indices = []
  for token in Corpus.tokenize(sentence):
    if token in self._words:
      index = word_list.index(token)
      indices.append(index)
  return indices
```

At this point we should have enough to validate our model using cross-validation. For that we will get into building the actual sentiment classifier as well as model validation.

Model Validation and the Sentiment Classifier

Now we can get to writing the cross-validation unit test, which will determine how well our classification works. We do this by having two different tests. The first has an error rate of 35% or less and ensures that when it trains and validates on the same data, there is zero error:

```
from fractions import Fraction
import unittest

import io
import os
from support_vector_machines.sentiment_classifier import SentimentClassifier


class TestSentimentClassifier(unittest.TestCase):
  def setUp(self):
    pass

  def test_validate(self):
    """cross validates with an error of 35% or less"""
    neg = self.split_file('data/rt-polaritydata/rt-polarity.neg')
    pos = self.split_file('data/rt-polaritydata/rt-polarity.pos')

    classifier = SentimentClassifier.build([
      neg['training'],
      pos['training']
    ])

    c = 2 ** 7
    classifier.c = c
    classifier.reset_model()

    n_er = self.validate(classifier, neg['validation'], 'negative')
    p_er = self.validate(classifier, pos['validation'], 'positive')
    total = Fraction(n_er.numerator + p_er.numerator,
                     n_er.denominator + p_er.denominator)
    print(total)
    self.assertLess(total, 0.35)

  def test_validate_itself(self):
    """yields a zero error when it uses itself"""
    classifier = SentimentClassifier.build([
      'data/rt-polaritydata/rt-polarity.neg',
      'data/rt-polaritydata/rt-polarity.pos'
    ])

    c = 2 ** 7
    classifier.c = c
    classifier.reset_model()

    n_er = self.validate(classifier,
```

```
                        'data/rt-polaritydata/rt-polarity.neg',
                        'negative')
    p_er = self.validate(classifier,
                         'data/rt-polaritydata/rt-polarity.pos',
                         'positive')
    total = Fraction(n_er.numerator + p_er.numerator,
                     n_er.denominator + p_er.denominator)
    print(total)
    self.assertEqual(total, 0)
```

In the second test we use two utility functions, which could also be achieved using either scikit-learn or other packages:

```
class TestSentimentClassifier(unittest.TestCase):
  # setUp
  # test_validate
  # test_validate_itself

  def validate(self, classifier, file, sentiment):
    total = 0
    misses = 0

    with(open(file, errors='ignore')) as f:
      for line in f:
        if classifier.classify(line) != sentiment:
          misses += 1
        total += 1
    return Fraction(misses, total)

  def split_file(self, filepath):
    ext = os.path.splitext(filepath)[1]
    counter = 0
    training_filename = 'tests/fixtures/training%s' % ext
    validation_filename = 'tests/fixtures/validation%s' % ext
    with(io.open(filepath, errors='ignore')) as input_file:
      with(io.open(validation_filename, 'w')) as val_file:
        with(io.open(training_filename, 'w')) as train_file:
          for line in input_file:
            if counter % 2 == 0:
              val_file.write(line)
            else:
              train_file.write(line)
            counter += 1
    return {'training': training_filename,
            'validation': validation_filename}
```

What this test does is validate that our model has a high enough accuracy to be useful.

Now we need to write our SentimentClassifier, which involves building a class that will respond to:

build

This class method will build a `SentimentClassifier` off of files instead of a `CorpusSet`.

present_answer

This method will take the numerical representation and output something useful to the end user.

c

This returns the C parameter that determines how wide the error bars are on SVMs.

reset_model

This resets the model.

words

This returns words.

fit_model

This does the big lifting and calls into the SVM library that scikit-learn wrote.

classify

This method classifies whether the string is negative or positive sentiment.

```
import io
import os

from numpy import ndarray

from sklearn import svm

from .corpus import Corpus
from .corpus_set import CorpusSet


class SentimentClassifier(object):
  ext_to_sentiment = {'.pos': 'positive',
                      '.neg': 'negative'}

  number_to_sentiment = {-1: 'negative',
                          1: 'positive'}

  @classmethod
  def present_answer(cls, answer):
    if isinstance(answer, ndarray):
      answer = answer[0]
    return cls.number_to_sentiment[answer]

  @classmethod
  def build(cls, files):
```

```
    corpora = []
    for file in files:
        ext = os.path.splitext(file)[1]
        corpus = Corpus(io.open(file, errors='ignore'),
                        cls.ext_to_sentiment[ext])
        corpora.append(corpus)
    corpus_set = CorpusSet(corpora)
    return SentimentClassifier(corpus_set)

def __init__(self, corpus_set):
    self._trained = False
    self._corpus_set = corpus_set
    self._c = 2 ** 7
    self._model = None

@property
def c(self):
    return self._c

@c.setter
def c(self, cc):
    self._c = cc

def reset_model(self):
    self._model = None

def words(self):
    return self._corpus_set.words

def classify(self, string):
    if self._model is None:
        self._model = self.fit_model()
    prediction = self._model.predict(self._corpus_set.feature_vector(string))
    return self.present_answer(prediction)

def fit_model(self):
    self._corpus_set.calculate_sparse_vectors()
    y_vec = self._corpus_set.yes
    x_mat = self._corpus_set.xes
    clf = svm.SVC(C=self.c,
                  cache_size=1000,
                  gamma=1.0 / len(y_vec),
                  kernel='linear',
                  tol=0.001)
    clf.fit(x_mat, y_vec)
    return clf
```

Up until this point we have discussed how to build the model but not about how to tune or verify the model. This is where a confusion matrix, precision, recall, and sensitivity analysis come into play.

Aggregating Sentiment

Now that we have a model that calculates sentiment from text, there's an additional issue of how to take multiple tickets per customer and map them to one measure of sentiment. There are a few ways of doing this:

- Mode
- Average (which would yield a score between –1 and 1)
- Exponential moving average

Each has benefits and downsides, so to explain the differences, let's take an example of a few customers with different sentiments (Table 7-1).

Table 7-1. Customer sentiment over time

Sequence number	Alice	Bob	Terry
1	1	–1	1
2	1	–1	1
3	1	–1	1
4	1	–1	–1
5	1	–1	–1
6	1	–1	1
7	–1	–1	1
8	–1	1	1
9	–1	1	1
10	–1	1	1

In general you can expect customers to change their minds over time. Alice was positive to begin with but became negative in her sentiment. Bob was negative in the beginning but became positive towards the end, and Terry was mostly positive but had some negative sentiment in there.

This brings up an interesting implementation detail. If we map these data to either a mode or average, then we will weight heavily things that are irrelevant. Alice is unhappy right now, while Bob is happy right now.

Mode and average are both fast implementations but there is another method called exponential weighted moving average or EWMA for short.

Exponentially Weighted Moving Average

Exponential moving averages are used heavily in finance since they weight recent data much heavier than old data. Things change quickly in finance and people can change as well. Unlike a normal average, this aims to change the weights from $\frac{1}{N}$ to some function that is based on a free parameter α, which tunes how much weight to give to the past.

So instead of the formula for a simple average being:

$$Y_{t+1} = \frac{Y_0 + Y_1 + \cdots + Y_t}{t}$$

we would use the formula:

$$Y_{t+1} = \alpha\left(Y_t + (1-\alpha)Y_{t-1} + (1-\alpha)^2 Y_{t-2} + (1-\alpha)^3 Y_{t-3} + \cdots\right)$$

This can be transformed into a recursive formula:

$$\hat{Y}_{t+1} = \alpha Y_t + (1-\alpha)\hat{Y}_t$$

Getting back to our original question on how to implement this let's look at the mode, average, and EWMA together (Table 7-2).

Table 7-2. Mode, average, and EWMA compared

Name	Mode	Average	EWMA ($\alpha = 0.94$)
Alice	1	0.2	−0.99997408
Bob	−1	−0.4	0.999568
Terry	1	0.6	0.99999845

As you can see EWMA maps our customers much better than a plain average or mode does. Alice is negative right now, Bob is positive now, and Terry has always been mostly positive.

Mapping Sentiment to Bottom Line

We've been able to build a model that takes textual data and splits it into two sentiment categories, either positive or negative. This is great! But it doesn't quite solve our problem, which originally was determining whether our customers were unhappy or not.

There is a certain amount of bias that one needs to avoid here: just because we have been able to map sentiment successfully into a given piece of text doesn't mean that we can tell whether the customer is happy or not. Causation isn't correlation, as they say, and vice versa.

But what can we do instead?

We can learn from this and understand our customers better, and also feed this data into other important algorithms, such as whether sentiment of text is correlated with more value from the customer or not (e.g., Figure 7-9).

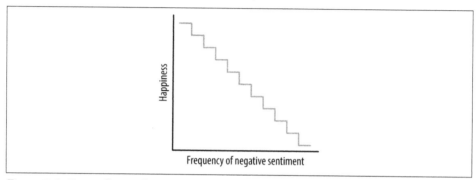

Figure 7-9. Generally speaking, the more complaints there are, the less happiness there is

This information is useful to running a business and improves our understanding of the data.

Conclusion

The SVM algorithm is very well suited to classifying two separable classes. It can be modified to separate more than two classes and doesn't suffer from the curse of dimensionality that KNN does. This chapter taught you how SVM can be used to separate happy and unhappy customers, as well as how to assign sentiment to movie data.

But more importantly, we've thought about how to go about testing our intuition of whether happy customers yield more money for our business.

## CHAPTER 8

Neural Networks

Humans are amazing pattern matchers. When we come out of the womb, we are able to make sense of the surrounding chaos until we have learned how to operate effectively in the world. This of course has to do with our upbringing, our environment, but most importantly our brain.

Your brain contains roughly 86 billion neurons that talk to one another over a network of synapses. These neurons are able to control your body functions as well as form thoughts, memories, and mental models. Each one of these neurons acts as part of a computer network, taking inputs and sending outputs to other neurons, all communicating in orchestrated fashion.

Mathematicians decided a long time ago it would be interesting to try to piece together mathematical representations of our brains, called neural networks. While the original research is over 60 years old, many of the techniques conceived back then still apply today and can be used to build models to tricky to compute problems.

In this chapter we will discuss neural networks in depth. We'll cover:

- Threshold logic, or how to build a Boolean function
- Neural networks as chaotic Boolean functions
- How to construct a feed-forward neural net
- Testing strategies for neural networks through gradient descent
- An example of classifying the language of handwritten text

What Is a Neural Network?

In a lot of ways neural networks are the perfect machine learning construct. They are a way of mapping inputs to a general output (see Figure 8-1).

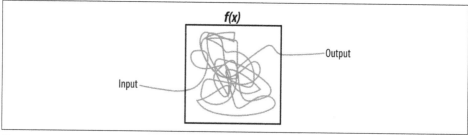

Figure 8-1. Neural networks: the perfect black box

What is great about neural networks is that, unlike perceptrons, they can be used to model complexity. So for instance if we have three inputs and one output we could arbitrarily set an interior complexity to 2 or 3 just based on our domain knowledge of the problem.

History of Neural Nets

When introduced, neural networks were about studying how the brain operates. Neurons in our brains work together in a network to process and make sense of inputs and stimuli. Alexander Bain and William James both proposed that brains operated in a network that could process lots of information. This network of neurons has the ability to recognize patterns and learn from previous data. For instance, if a child is shown a picture of eight dogs, she starts to understand what a dog looks like.

This research was expanded to include a more artificial bent when Warren McCulloch and Walter Pitts invented threshold logic. Threshold logic combines binary information to determine logical truth. They suggested using something called a step function, which attached a threshold to either accept or reject a summation of previous information. After many years of research, neural networks and threshold logic were combined to form what we call an artificial neural network.

Boolean Logic

As programmers, we're constantly dealing with Boolean functions, which return either yes or no (true or false). Another way of thinking about Boolean data is to encode yes or no with binary bits (0 for false, 1 for true).

This is such a common occurrence that there already exist many functions that deal with Boolean data. Functions such as OR, AND, NAND, NOR, and NOT are all Boolean functions. They take in two inputs that are true or false and output something that is true or false.

These have been used for great advances in the electronics community through digital logic gates and can be composed together to solve many problems. But how would we go about constructing something like this?

A simple example of modeling the OR function would be the following:

$$OR(a, b) = \min(1, a + b)$$

Perceptrons

Perceptrons take the idea of Boolean logic even further to include more fuzzy logic. They usually involve returning a value based on a threshold being met or not. Let's say that you're a teacher and you wish to assign pass/fail grades to your students at the end of the quarter. Obviously you need to come up with a way of cutting off the people who failed from the ones who didn't. This can be quite subjective but usually follows a general procedure of:

```python
def threshold(x):
  if sum(weights * x) + b > 0.5:
    return 1
  else:
    return 0
```

x is a vector of all the grades you collected the entire quarter and weights is a vector of weightings. For instance, you might want to weight the final grade higher. b is just a freebie to the students for showing up.

Using such a simple formula we could traverse the optimal weightings by determining a priori how many people we'd like to fail. Let's say we have 100 students and only want to fail the bottom 10%. This goal is something we can actually code.

How to Construct Feed-Forward Neural Nets

There are many different kinds of neural networks, but this chapter will focus on feed-forward networks and recurrent networks.

What makes neural networks special is their use of a hidden layer of weighted functions called neurons, with which you can effectively build a network that maps a lot of other functions (Figure 8-2). Without a hidden layer of functions, neural networks would be just a set of simple weighted functions.

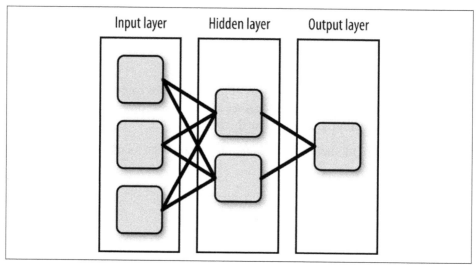

Figure 8-2. A feed-forward network

Neural networks are denoted by the number of neurons per layer. For example, if we have 20 neurons in our input layer, 10 in one hidden layer, and 5 in an output layer, it would be a 20-10-5 network. If there is more than one hidden layer, then we would denote it as, say, 20-7-7-5 (the two middle 7s are layers with 7 nodes apiece).

To summarize, then, neural networks comprise the following parts:

- The input layer
- The hidden layer(s)
- Neurons
- The output layer
- The training algorithm

Next, I'll explain what each of these parts does and how it works.

Input Layer

The input layer, shown in Figure 8-3, is the entry point of a neural network. It is the entry point for the inputs you are giving to the model. There are no neurons in this layer because its main purpose is to serve as a conduit to the hidden layer(s). The input type is important, as neural networks work with only two types: symmetric or standard.

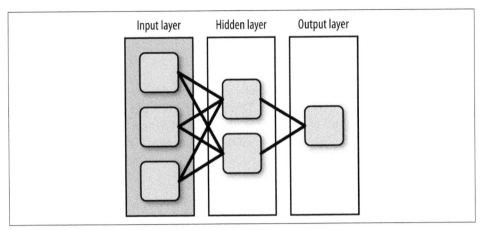

Figure 8-3. Input layer of neural network

When training a neural network, we have observations and inputs. Taking the simple example of an exclusive OR (also known as XOR), we have the truth table shown in Table 8-1.

Table 8-1. XOR truth

A	B	XOR(A,B)
0	0	0
0	1	1
1	0	1
1	1	0

Another way of representing XOR is to look at a Venn diagram (Figure 8-4). Given two sets of data, the shaded area shows the XOR area. Notice that the middle is empty.

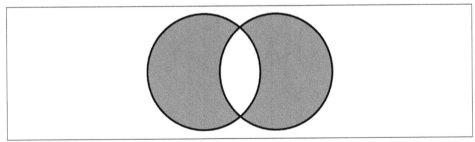

Figure 8-4. XOR function in a Venn diagram (Source: Wikimedia)

In this case, we have four observations and two inputs, which could either be true or false. Neural networks do not work off of true or false, though, and knowing how to code the input is key. We'll need to translate these to either standard or symmetric inputs.

Standard inputs

The standard range for input values is between 0 and 1. In our previous XOR example, we would code true as 1 and false as 0. This style of input has one downside: if your data is sparse, meaning full of 0s, it can skew results. Having a data set with lots of 0s means we risk the model breaking down. Only use standard inputs if you know that there isn't sparse data.

Symmetric inputs

Symmetric inputs avoid the issue with 0s. These are between −1 and 1. In our preceding example, −1 would be false, and 1 would be true. This kind of input has the benefit of our model not breaking down because of the zeroing-out effect. In addition to that, it puts less emphasis on the middle of a distribution of inputs. If we introduced a *maybe* into the XOR calculation, we could map that as 0 and ignore it. Inputs can be used in either the symmetric or standard format but need to be marked as such, because the way we calculate the output of neurons depends on this.

Hidden Layers

Without hidden layers, neural networks would be a set of weighted linear combinations. In other words, hidden layers permit neural networks to model nonlinear data (Figure 8-5).

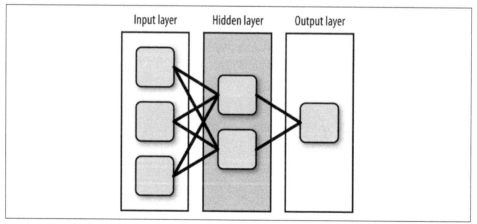

Figure 8-5. The hidden layer of a network

Each hidden layer contains a set of neurons (Figure 8-6), which then pass to the output layer.

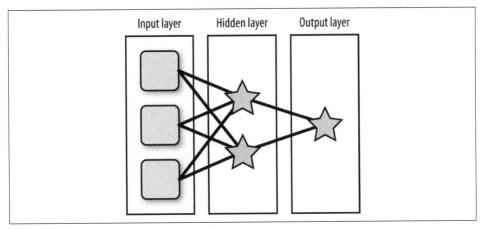

Figure 8-6. The neurons of the network

Neurons

Neurons are weighted linear combinations that are wrapped in an activation function. The weighted linear combination (or sum) is a way of aggregating all of the previous neurons' data into one output for the next layer to consume as input. Activation functions, shown in Figures 8-7 through 8-11, serve as a way to normalize data so it's either symmetric or standard.

As a network is feeding information forward, it is aggregating previous inputs into weighted sums. We take the value y and compute the activated value based on an activation function.

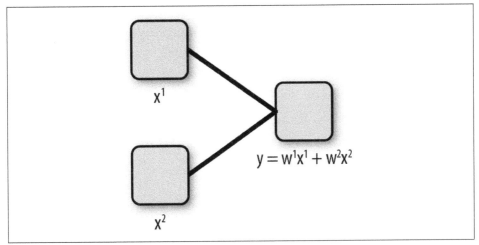

Figure 8-7. A neuron is a summation of previous inputs

Activation Functions

As mentioned, activation functions, some of which are listed in Table 8-2, serve as a way to normalize data between either the standard or symmetric ranges. They also are differentiable, and need to be, because of how we find weights in a training algorithm.

Table 8-2. Activation functions

Name	Standard	Symmetric
Sigmoid	$\dfrac{1}{1+e^{-2 \cdot sum}}$	$\dfrac{2}{1+e^{-2 \cdot sum}} - 1$
Cosine	$\dfrac{\cos(sum)}{2} + 0.5$	$\cos(sum)$
Sine	$\dfrac{\sin(sum)}{2} + 0.5$	$\sin(sum)$
Gaussian	$\dfrac{1}{e^{sum^2}}$	$\dfrac{2}{e^{sum^2}} - 1$
Elliott	$\dfrac{0.5 \cdot sum}{1 + |sum|} + 0.5$	$\dfrac{sum}{1 + |sum|}$
Linear	$sum > 1 ? 1 : (sum < 0 : sum)$	$sum > 1 ? 1 : (sum < -1 ? -1 : sum)$
Threshold	$sum < 0 ? 0 : 1$	$sum < 0 ? -1 : 1$

The big advantage of using activation functions is that they serve as a way of buffering incoming values at each layer. This is useful because neural networks have a way of finding patterns and forgetting about the noise. There are two main categories for activation functions: sloped or periodic. In most cases, the sloped activation functions (shown in Figures 8-8 and 8-10) are a suitable default choice. The periodic functions (shown in Figures 8-9 and 8-11) are used for modeling data with lots of noise. They generally take the form of either a sine or cosine function.

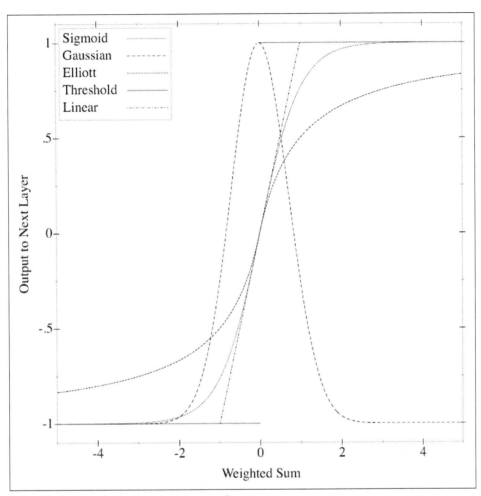

Figure 8-8. Symmetric sloped activation functions

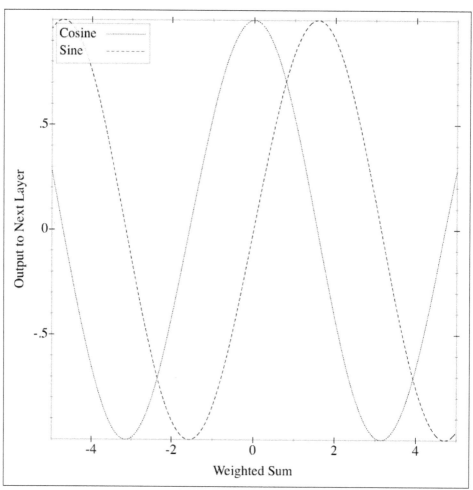

Figure 8-9. Symmetric periodic activation functions

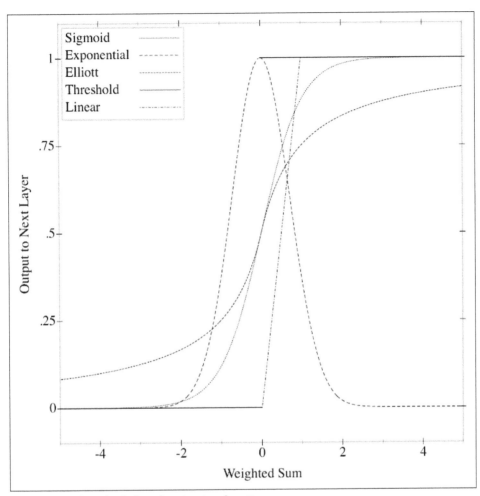

Figure 8-10. Standard sloped activation functions

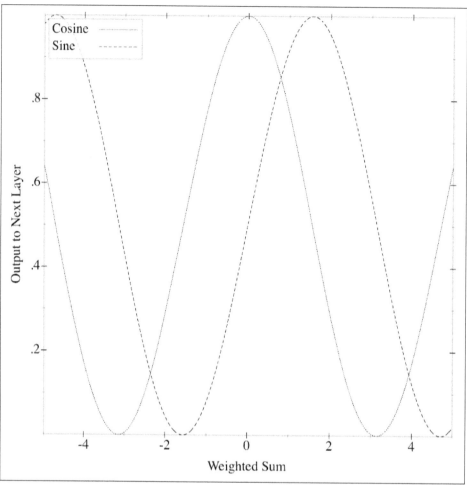

Figure 8-11. Standard periodic activation functions

Sigmoid is the default function to be used with neurons because of its ability to smooth out the decision. Elliott is a sigmoidal function that is quicker to compute, so it's the choice I make. Cosine and sine waves are used when you are mapping something that has a random-looking process associated with it. In most cases, these trigonometric functions aren't as useful to our problems. Neurons are where all of the work is done. They are a weighted sum of previous inputs put through an activation function that either bounds it to 0 to 1 or –1 to 1. In the case of a neuron where we have two inputs before it, the function for the neuron would be $y = \phi(w_1 \dot{x}_1 + w_2 \dot{x}_2)$, where ϕ is an activation function like sigmoid, and w_i are weights determined by a training algorithm.

Output Layer

The output layer is similar to the input layer except that it has neurons in it. This is where the data comes out of the model. Just as with the input layer, this data will either be symmetric or standard. Output layers decide how many neurons are output, which is a function of what we're modeling (see Figure 8-12). In the case of a function that outputs whether a stop light is red, green, or yellow, we'd have three outputs (one for each color). Each of those outputs would contain an approximation for what we want.

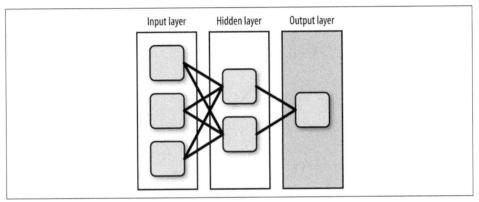

Figure 8-12. The output layer of the network

Training Algorithms

As mentioned, the weights for each neuron came from a training algorithm. There are many such algorithms, but the most common are:

- Back propagation
- QuickProp
- RProp

All of these algorithms find optimal weights for each neuron. They do so through *iterations*, also known as *epochs*. For each epoch, a training algorithm goes through the entire neural network and compares it against what is expected. At this point, it learns from past miscalculations.

These algorithms have one thing in common: they are trying to find the optimal solution in a convex error surface. You can think of convex error surface as a bowl with a minimum value in it. Imagine that you are at the top of a hill and want to make it to a valley, but the valley is full of trees. You can't see much in front of you, but you know that you want to get to the valley. You would do so by proceeding based on local inputs and guessing where you want to go next. This is known as the *gradient descent algorithm* (i.e., determining minimum error by walking down a valley) and it is illustrated in Figure 8-13. The training algorithms do the same thing; they are looking to minimize error by using local information.

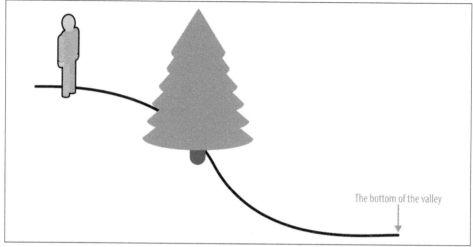

Figure 8-13. Gradient descent down a valley

The Delta Rule

While we could solve a massive amount of equations, it would be faster to iterate. Instead of trying to calculate the derivative of the error function with respect to the weight, we calculate a change in weight for each neuron's weights. This is known as the *delta rule*, and it is as follows:

Equation 8-1. Delta rule

$$\Delta w_{ji} = \alpha \left(t_j - \phi(h_j) \right) \phi'(h_j) x_i$$

This states that the change in weight for neuron *j*'s weight number *i* is:

```
alpha * (expected - calculated) * derivative_of_calculated * input_at_i
```

α is the learning rate and is a small constant. This initial idea, though, is what powers the idea behind the *back propagation* algorithm, or the general case of the delta rule.

Back Propagation

Back propagation is the simplest of the three algorithms that determine the weight of a neuron. You define error as (*expected * actual*)^2 where *expected* is the expected out-

---

put and *actual* is the calculated number from the neurons. We want to find where the derivative of that equals 0, which is the minimum.

Equation 8-2. Back propagation

$$\Delta w(t) = -\alpha(t-y)\phi'x_i + \epsilon\Delta w(t-1)$$

ϵ is the momentum factor and propels previous weight changes into our current weight change, whereas α is the learning rate.

Back propagation has the disadvantage of taking many epochs to calculate. Up until 1988, researchers were struggling to train simple neural networks. Their research on how to improve this led to a whole new algorithm called QuickProp.

QuickProp

Scott Fahlman introduced the QuickProp algorithm after he studied how to improve back propagation. He asserted that back propagation took too long to converge to a solution. He proposed that we instead take the biggest steps without overstepping the solution.

Fahlman determined that there are two ways to improve back propagation: making the momentum and learning rate dynamic, and making use of a second derivative of the error with respect to each weight. In the first case, you could better optimize for each weight, and in the second case, you could utilize Newton's method of approximating functions.

With QuickProp, the main difference from back propagation is that you keep a copy of the error derivative computed during the previous epoch, along with the difference between the current and previous values of this weight.

To calculate a weight change at time t, use the following function:

$$\Delta w(t) = \frac{S(t)}{S(t-1)-S(t)}\Delta w(t-1)$$

This carries the risk of changing the weights too much, so there is a new parameter for maximum growth. No weight is allowed to be greater in magnitude than the maximum growth rate multiplied by the previous step for that weight.

RProp

RProp is a good algorithm because it converges quicker. It was introduced by Martin Riedmiller in the 1990s and has been improved since then. It converges on a solution quickly due to its insight that the algorithm can update the weights many times through an epoch. Instead of calculating weight changes based on a formula, it uses only the sign for change as well as an increase factor and decrease factor.

To see what this algorithm looks like in code, we need to define a few constants (or defaults). These are a way to make sure the algorithm doesn't operate forever or become volatile. These defaults were taken from the FANN library.

The basic algorithm is easier to explain in Python instead of writing out the partial derivatives. For ease of reading, note that I am not calculating the error gradients (i.e., the change in error with respect to that specific weight term). This code gives you an idea of how the RProp algorithm works using just pure Python code:

```python
import numpy as np
import random

neurons = 3
inputs = 4

delta_zero = 0.1
increase_factor = 1.2
decrease_factor = 0.5
delta_max = 50.0
delta_min = 0
max_epoch = 100
deltas = np.zeros((inputs, neurons))
last_gradient = np.zeros((inputs, neurons))


def sign(x):
 if x > 0:
  return 1
 elif x < 0:
  return -1
 else:
  return 0

weights = [random.uniform(-1, 1) for _ in range(inputs)]
for j in range(max_epoch):
  for i, weight in enumerate(weights):
    # Current gradient is derived from the change of each value at each layer
    # Do note that we haven't derived current_gradient since that would detract
    # from the example

    gradient_momentum = last_gradient[i][j] * current_gradient[i][j]

    if gradient_momentum > 0:
      deltas[i][j] = min(deltas[i][j] * increase_factor, delta_max)
      change_weight = -sign(current_gradient[i][j]) * deltas[i][j]
      last_gradient[i][j] = current_gradient[i][j]
    elif gradient_momentum < 0:
      deltas[i][j] = max(deltas[i][j] * decrease_factor, delta_min)
```

```
        last_gradient[i][j] = 0
      else:
        change_weight = -sign(current_gradient[i][j])* deltas[i][j]
        weights[i] = weights[i] + change_weight

      last_gradient[i][j] = current_gradient[i][j]
```

These are the fundamentals you need to understand to be able to build a neural network. Next, we'll talk about how to do so, and what decisions we must make to build an effective one.

Building Neural Networks

Before you begin building a neural network, you must answer the following questions:

- How many hidden layers should you use?
- How many neurons per layer?
- What is your tolerance for error?

How Many Hidden Layers?

As noted earlier in this chapter, what makes neural networks unique is their usage of hidden layers. If you took out hidden layers, you'd have a linear combination problem.

You aren't bound to use any number of hidden layers, but there are three heuristics that help:

- Do not use more than two hidden layers; otherwise, you might overfit the data. With too many layers, the network starts to memorize the training data. Instead, we want it to find patterns.
- One hidden layer will do the job of approximating a continuous mapping. This is the common case. Most neural networks have only one hidden layer in them.
- Two hidden layers will be able to push past a continuous mapping. This is an uncommon case, but if you know that you don't have a continuous mapping, you can use two hidden layers.

There is no steadfast rule holding you to these heuristics for picking the number of hidden layers. It comes down to trying to minimize the risk of overfitting or underfitting your data.

How Many Neurons for Each Layer?

Neural networks are excellent aggregators and terrible expanders. Neurons themselves are weighted sums of previous neurons, so they have a tendency to not expand out as well as they combine. If you think about it, a hidden layer of 2 that goes to an output layer of 30 would mean that for each output neuron, there would be two inputs. There just isn't enough entropy or data to make a well-fitted model.

This idea of emphasizing aggregation over expansion leads us to the next set of heuristics:

- The number of hidden neurons should be between the number of inputs and the number of neurons at the output layer.

- The number of hidden neurons should be two-thirds the size of the input layer, plus the size of the output layer.

- The number of hidden neurons should be less than twice the size of the input layer.

This comes down to trial and error, though, as the number of hidden neurons will influence how well the model cross-validates, as well as the convergence on a solution. This is just a starting point.

Tolerance for Error and Max Epochs

The tolerance for error gives us a time to stop training. We will never get to a perfect solution but rather converge on one. If you want an algorithm that performs well, then the error rate might be low, like 0.01%. But in most cases, that will take a long time to train due to its intolerance for error.

Many start with an error tolerance of 1%. Through cross-validation, this might need to be tightened even more. In neural network parlance, the tolerance is internal, is measured as a mean squared error, and defines a stopping place for the network.

Neural networks are trained over epochs, and this is set before the training algorithm even starts. If an algorithm is taking 10,000 iterations to get to a solution, then there might be a high risk for overtraining and creating a sensitive network. A starting point for training is 1,000 epochs or iterations to train over. This way, you can model some complexity without getting too carried away.

Both max epochs and maximum error define our converging points. They serve as a way to signal when the training algorithm can stop and yield the neural network. At this point, we've learned enough to get our hands dirty and try a real-world example.

Using a Neural Network to Classify a Language

Characters used in a language have a direct correlation with the language itself. Mandarin is recognizable due to its characters, because each character means a specific word. This correlation is true of many Latin-based languages, but in regards to letter frequency.

If we look at the difference of "The quick brown fox jumped over the lazy dog" in English and its German equivalent, "Der schnelle braune Fuchs sprang über den faulen Hund," we'd get the frequency chart shown in Table 8-3.

Table 8-3. Difference in letter frequency between English and German sentence

	a	b	c	d	e	f	g	h	i	j	k	l	m	n	o	p	q	r	s	t	u	v	w	x	y	z	ü
English	1	1	1	2	4	1	1	2	1	1	1	1	1	1	4	1	1	2	0	2	2	1	1	1	1	1	0
German	3	2	2	3	7	2	1	3	0	0	0	3	0	6	0	1	0	4	2	0	4	0	0	0	0	1	1
Difference	2	1	1	1	3	1	0	1	1	1	1	2	1	5	4	0	1	2	2	2	2	1	1	1	1	0	1

There is a subtle difference between German and English. German uses quite a few more Ns, whereas English uses a lot of Os. If we wanted to expand this to a few more European languages, how would we do that? More specifically, how can we build a model to classify sentences written in English, Polish, German, Finnish, Swedish, or Norwegian?

In this case, we'll build a simple model to predict a language based on the frequency of the characters in the sentences. But before we start, we need to have some data. For that, we'll use the most translated book in the world: the Bible. Let's extract all the chapters out of Matthew and Acts.

The approach we will take is to extract all the sentences out of these text files and create vectors of frequency normalized between 0 and 1. From that, we will train a network that will take those inputs and then match them to a vector of 6. The vector of 6 is defined as the index of the language equaling 1. If the language we are using to train is index 3, the vector would look like [0,0,0,1,0,0] (zero-based indexing).

Setup Notes

All of the code we're using for this example can be found on GitHub (*https:// github.com/thoughtfulml/examples-in-python/tree/master/artificial-neural-networks*).

Python is constantly changing, so the README file is the best place to get up to speed on running the examples.

Coding and Testing Design

The overall approach we will be taking is to write two classes to parse the Bible verses and train a neural network:

Language
  This class will parse the Bible verses and calculate a frequency of letter occurences.

Network
  This will take language training data and build a network that calculates the most likely language attached to new incoming text (see Figure 8-14).

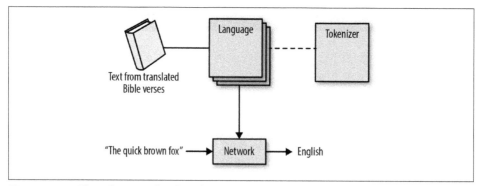

Figure 8-14. Class diagram for classifying text to languages

The testing for our neural network will focus primarily on testing the data transmission into theanets, which we will test using a cross-validation test. We will set a threshold for acceptance as a unit test and use that to test.

The Data

The data was grabbed from biblegateway.com. To have a good list of data I've downloaded passages in English, Polish, German, Finnish, Swedish, and Norwegian. They are from the books Acts and Matthew. The script I used to download the data was written in Ruby and I felt that it wouldn't be helpful to put it in here translated. Feel free to check out the script at *https://github.com/thoughtfulml/examples/blob/master/6-neural-networks/script/grab_bible.rb* if you'd like.

Writing the Seam Test for Language

To take our training data, we need to build a class to parse that and interface with our neural network. For that, we will use the class name Language. Its purpose is to take a file of text in a given language and load it into a distribution of character frequencies.

When needed, `Language` will output a vector of these characters, all summing up to 1. All of our inputs will be between 0 and 1. Our parameters are:

- We want to make sure that our data is correct and sums to 1.
- We don't want characters like UTF-8 spaces or punctuation entering our data.
- We want to downcase all characters. *A* should be translated as *a*. *Ü* should also be *ü*.

This helps us to make sure that our `Language` class, which takes a text file and outputs an array of hashes, is correct:

```
# coding=utf-8
import string
import unittest

from io import StringIO
from artificial_neural_networks.language import Language


class TestLanguage(unittest.TestCase):
  def setUp(self):
    self.language_data = u'''
abcdefghijklmnopqrstuvwxyz.
ABCDEFGHIJKLMNOPQRSTUVWXYZ.
\u00A0.
!~@#$%^&*()_+'?[]""''—<>»«›‹-„/.
ïëéüòèöÄÖßÜøæåÅØóąłżźśęńśćź.
'''
    self.special_characters = self.language_data.split("\n")[-1].strip()
    self.language_io = StringIO(self.language_data)
    self.language = Language(self.language_io, 'English')

  def test_keys(self):
    """has the proper keys for each vector"""
    self.assertListEqual(list(string.ascii_lowercase),
                         sorted(self.language.vectors[0].keys()))
    self.assertListEqual(list(string.ascii_lowercase),
                         sorted(self.language.vectors[1].keys()))

    special_chars = sorted(set(u'ïëéüòèöäößüøæåÅøóąłżźśęńśćź'))
    self.assertListEqual(special_chars,
                         sorted(self.language.vectors[-1].keys()))

  def test_values(self):
    """sums to 1 for all vectors"""
    for vector in self.language.vectors:
      self.assertEqual(1, sum(vector.values()))

  def test_character_set(self):
    """returns characters that is a unique set of characters used"""
```

```
chars = list(string.ascii_lowercase)
chars += list(set(u'ïëéüòèöäößüøæåàóąłżźśęńśćź'))

self.assertListEqual(sorted(chars),
                     sorted(self.language.characters))
```

At this point, we have not written Language, and all of our tests fail. For the first goal, let's get something that counts all the alpha characters and stops on a sentence. That would look like this:

```
from .tokenizer import Tokenizer


class Language(object):
  def __init__(self, io, name):
    self._name = name
    self._vectors, self._characters = Tokenizer.tokenize(io)

  @property
  def name(self): return self._name

  @property
  def vectors(self): return self._vectors

  @property
  def characters(self): return self._characters

# coding=utf-8
from fractions import Fraction

import collections


class Tokenizer(object):
  punctuation = list(u'~@#$%^&*()_+\'[]""''—<>»«›‹-„/')
  spaces = list(u' \u00A0\n')
  stop_characters = list('.?!')

  @classmethod
  def tokenize(cls, io):
    vectors = []
    dist = collections.defaultdict(int)
    characters = set()

    for char in io.read():
      if char in cls.stop_characters:
        if len(dist) > 0:
          vectors.append(cls.normalize(dist))
          dist = collections.defaultdict(int)
      elif char not in cls.spaces and char not in cls.punctuation:
        character = char.lower()
        characters.add(character)
        dist[character] += 1
```

```
if len(dist) > 0:
    vectors.append(cls.normalize(dist))

return vectors, characters
```

Now we have something that should work. Do note that there is the Unicode space here, which is denoted as \u00a0.

Now we have a new problem, though, which is that the data does not add up to 1. We will introduce a new function, normalize, which takes a hash of values and applies the function x/sum(x) to all values. Note that I used Fraction, which increases the reliability of calculations and doesn't do floating-point arithmetic until needed:

```
class Tokenizer(object):
    # tokenize

    @classmethod
    def normalize(cls, dist):
        sum_values = sum(dist.values())
        return {k: Fraction(v, sum_values) for k, v in dist.items()}
```

Everything is green and things look great for Language. We have full test coverage on a class that will be used to interface with our neural network. Now we can move on to building a Network class.

Cross-Validating Our Way to a Network Class

I used the Bible to find training *data* for our language classification because it is the most translated book in history. For the data, I decided to download Matthew and Acts in English, Finnish, German, Norwegian, Polish, and Swedish. With this natural divide between Acts and Matthew, we can define 12 tests of a model trained with Acts and see how it compares to Matthew's data, and vice versa.

The code looks like:

```
# coding=utf-8
from glob import glob
import unittest

from io import StringIO
import codecs
import os
import re
from nose_parameterized import parameterized
from artificial_neural_networks.language import Language
from artificial_neural_networks.network import Network


def language_name(file_name):
    basename, ext = os.path.splitext(os.path.basename(file_name))
    return basename.split('_')[0]
```

```
def load_glob(pattern):
  result = []
  for file_name in glob(pattern):
    result.append(Language(codecs.open(file_name, encoding='utf-8'),
                           language_name(file_name)))
  return result


class TestNetwork(unittest.TestCase):
  matthew_languages = load_glob('data/*_0.txt')
  acts_languages = load_glob('data/*_1.txt')
  matthew_verses = Network(matthew_languages)
  matthew_verses.train()
  acts_verses = Network(acts_languages)
  acts_verses.train()

  @parameterized.expand('English Finnish German Norwegian Polish Swedish'.split())
  def test_accuracy(self, lang):
    """Trains and cross-validates with an error of 5%"""
    print('Test for %s' % lang)
    self.compare(self.matthew_verses, './data/%s_1.txt' % lang)
    self.compare(self.acts_verses, './data/%s_0.txt' % lang)

  def compare(self, network, file_name):
    misses = 0.0
    hits = 0.0
    with codecs.open(file_name, encoding='utf-8') as f:
      text = f.read()

    for sentence in re.split(r'[\.!\?]', text):
      language = network.predict(StringIO(sentence))
      if language is None: continue
      if language.name == language_name(file_name):
        hits += 1
      else:
        misses += 1

    total = misses + hits

    self.assertLess(misses,
                    0.05 * total,
                    msg='%s has failed with a miss rate of %f' % (file_name,
                                                     misses / total))
```

There is a folder called *data* in the root of the project that contains files in the form *Language_0.txt* and *Language_1.txt* where *Language* is the language name, *_0* is the index mapping to Matthew, and *_1* is the index mapping to Acts.

It takes a while to train a neural network, depending, so that is why we are only cross-validating with two folds. At this point, we have 12 tests defined. Of course, nothing will work now because we haven't written the `Network` class. To start out the `Network` class we define an initial class as taking an array of `Language` classes. Secondly, because we don't want to write all the neural network by hand, we're using a library called Theanets. Our main goal initially is to get a neural network to accept and train.

But now we have an important decision to make: which neural net library should we use? There are many out there, and of course we *could* build our own. Probably the best one out there right now is theanets, which integrates nicely with NumPy and can actually be utilized for deep learning, autoencoding, and much more than just straight feed-forward networks. We will use that, although you could use other libraries like Theanets.

```python
import numpy as np
import theanets
import climate

from .tokenizer import Tokenizer

climate.enable_default_logging()

class Network(object):
  def __init__(self, languages, error=0.005):
    self._trainer = None
    self._net = None
    self.languages = languages
    self.error = error
    self.inputs = set()
    for language in languages:
      self.inputs.update(language.characters)
    self.inputs = sorted(self.inputs)

  def _build_trainer(self):
    inputs = []
    desired_outputs = []
    for language_index, language in enumerate(self.languages):
      for vector in language.vectors:
        inputs.append(self._code(vector))
        desired_outputs.append(language_index)
    inputs = np.array(inputs, dtype=np.float32)
    desired_outputs = np.array(desired_outputs, dtype=np.int32)
    self._trainer = (inputs, desired_outputs)

  def _code(self, vector):
    result = np.zeros(len(self.inputs))
    for char, freq in vector.items():
      if char in self.inputs:
        result[self.inputs.index(char)] = float(freq)
    return result

  def _build_ann(self):
    hidden_neurons = 2 * (len(self.inputs) + len(self.languages)) / 3
```

```
parameters = [len(self.inputs),
              {'size': int(hidden_neurons), 'activation': 'tanh'},
              len(self.languages)]

self._net = theanets.Classifier(parameters)
```

Now that we have the proper inputs and the proper outputs, the model is set up and we should be able to run the whole *crossvalidation.py*. But, of course, there is an error because we cannot run new data against the network. To address this, we need to build a function called #run. At this point, we have something that works and looks like this:

```
class Network(object):
  # __init__
  # _build_trainer
  # _code
  # _build_ann

  def train(self):
    self._build_trainer()
    self._build_ann()
    self._net.train(self._trainer, learning_rate=0.01)

  def predict(self, sentence):
    if self._net is None or self._trainer is None:
      raise Exception('Must train first')
    vectors, characters = Tokenizer.tokenize(sentence)
    if len(vectors) == 0:
      return None
    input = np.array(self._code(vectors[0]),
                     ndmin=2,
                     dtype=np.float32)
    result = self._net.predict(input)
    return self.languages[result[0]]
```

Tuning the Neural Network

At this point there's quite a few optimizations we could make. Also you could play around with different hidden-layer activation functions like tanh, softmax, or various others.

I'll leave further tuning to you as an exercise in playing around with what works and what does not. You can try many different activation functions, as well as internal rates of decay or errors. The takeaway here is that with an initial test to base accuracy against, you can try many different avenues.

Precision and Recall for Neural Networks

Going a step further, when we deploy this neural network code to a production environment, we need to close the information loop by introducing a precision and recall metric to track over time. This metric will be calculated from user input.

We can measure precision and recall by asking in our user interface whether our prediction was correct. From this text, we can capture the blurb and the correct classification, and feed that back into our model the next time we train.

To learn more about monitoring precision and recall, see Chapter 5.

What we need to monitor the performance of this neural network in production is a metric for how many times a classification was run, as well as how many times it was wrong.

Wrap-Up of Example

The neural networks algorithm is a fun way of mapping information and learning through iterations, and it works well for our case of mapping sentences to languages. Loading this code in an IPython session, I had fun trying out phrases like "meep moop," which is classified as Norwegian! Feel free to play with the code.

Conclusion

The neural networks algorithm is a powerful tool in a machine learning toolkit. Neural networks serve as a way of mapping previous observations through a functional model. While they are touted as black box models, they can be understood with a little bit of mathematics and illustration. You can use neural networks for many things, like mapping letter frequencies to languages or handwriting detection. There are many problems being worked on right now with regards to this algorithm, and several in-depth books have been written on the topic as well. Anything written by Geoffrey Hinton is worth a read, namely *Unsupervised Learning: Foundations of Neural Computation*.

This chapter introduced neural networks as an artificial version of our brain and explained how they work by summing up inputs using a weighted function. These weighted functions were then normalized within a certain range. Many algorithms exist to train these weight values, but the most prevalent is the RProp algorithm. Last, we summed it all up with a practical example of mapping sentences to languages.

## CHAPTER 9

Clustering

Up until this point we have been solving problems of fitting a function to a set of data. For instance, given previously observed mushroom attributes and edibleness, how would we classify new mushrooms? Or, given a neighborhood, what should the house value be?

This chapter talks about a completely different learning problem: clustering. This is a subset of unsupervised learning methods and is useful in practice for understanding data at its core.

If you've been to a library you've seen clustering at work. The Dewey Decimal system is a form of clustering. Dewey came up with a system that attached numbers of increasing granularity to categories of books, and it revolutionized libraries.

We will talk about what it means to be unsupervised and what power exists in that, as well as two clustering algorithms: K-Means and expectation maximization (EM) clustering. We will also address two other issues associated with clustering and unsupervised learning:

- How do you test a clustering algorithm?
- The impossibility theorem.

Studying Data Without Any Bias

If I were to give you an Excel spreadsheet full of data, and instead of giving you any idea as to what I'm looking for, just asked you to tell me something, what could you tell me? That is what unsupervised learning aims to do: study what the data is about.

A more formal definition would be to think of unsupervised learning as finding the best function f such that $f(x) = x$. At first glance, wouldn't $x = x$? But it's more than just that—you can always map data onto itself—but what unsupervised learning does is define a function that describes the data.

What does that mean?

Unsupervised learning is trying to find a function that generalizes the data to some degree. So instead of trying to fit it to some classification or number, instead we are just fitting the function to describe the data. This is essential to understand since it gives us a glimpse as to how to test this.

Let's dive into an example.

User Cohorts

Grouping people into cohorts makes a lot of business and marketing sense. For instance, your first customer is different from your ten thousandth customer or your millionth customer. This problem of defining users into *cohorts* is a common one. If we were able to effectively split our customers into different buckets based on behavior and time of signup, then we could better serve them by diversifying our marketing strategy.

The problem is that we don't have a predefined label for customer cohorts. To get over this problem you could look at what month and year they became a customer. But that is making a big assumption about that being the defining factor that splits customers into groups. What if time of first purchase had nothing to do with whether they were in one cohort or the other? For example, they could only have made one purchase or many.

Instead, what can we learn from the data? Take a look at Table 9-1. Let's say we know when they signed up, how much they've spent, and what their favorite color is. Assume also that over the last two years we've only had 10 users sign up (well, I hope you have more than that over two years, but let's keep this simple).

Table 9-1. Data collected over 2 years

User ID	Signup date	Money spent	Favorite color
1	Jan 14	40	N/A
2	Nov 3	50	Orange
3	Jan 30	53	Green
4	Oct 3	100	Magenta
5	Feb 1	0	Cyan
6	Dec 31	0	Purple
7	Sep 3	0	Mauve

User ID	Signup date	Money spent	Favorite color
8	Dec 31	0	Yellow
9	Jan 13	14	Blue
10	Jan 1	50	Beige

Given these data, we want to learn a function that describes what we have. Looking at these rows, you notice that the favorite colors are irrelevant data. There is no information as to whether users should be in a cohort. That leaves us with *Money spent* and *Signup date*. There seems to be a group of users who spend money, and one of those who don't. That is useful information. In the *Signup date* column you'll notice that there are a lot of users who sign up around the beginning of the year and end of the previous one, as well as around September, October, or November.

Now we have a choice: whether we want to find the gist of this data in something compact or find a new mapping of this data onto a transformation. Remember the discussion of kernel tricks in Chapter 7? This is all we're doing—mapping this data onto a new dimension. For the purposes of this chapter we will delve into a new mapping technique: in Chapter 10, on data extraction and improvement, we'll delve into compaction of data.

Let's imagine that we have 10 users in our database and have information on when they signed up, and how much money they spent. Our marketing team has assigned them manually to cohorts (Table 9-2).

Table 9-2. Manual cohort assignment to the original data set

User ID	Signup date (days to Jan 1)	Money spent	Cohort
1	Jan 14 (13)	40	1
2	Nov 3 (59)	50	2
3	Jan 30 (29)	53	1
4	Oct 3 (90)	100	2
5	Feb 1 (31)	0	1
6	Dec 31 (1)	0	1
7	Sep 3 (120)	0	2
8	Dec 31 (1)	0	1
9	Jan 13 (12)	14	1
10	Jan 1 (0)	50	1

We have divided the group into two groups where seven users are in group 1, which we could call the beginning-of-the-year signups, and end-of-the-year signups are in group 2.

But there's something here that doesn't sit well. We assigned the users to different clusters, but didn't really test anything—what to do?

Testing Cluster Mappings

Testing unsupervised methods doesn't have a good tool such as cross-validation, confusion matrices, ROC curves, or sensitivity analysis, but they still can be tested, using one of these two methods:

- Determining some a priori fitness of the unsupervised learning method
- Comparing results to some sort of ground truth

Fitness of a Cluster

Domain knowledge can become very useful in determining the fitness of an unsupervised model. For instance, if we want to find things that are similar, we might use some sort of distance-based metric. If instead we wish to determine independent factors of the data, we might calculate fitness based on correlation or covariance.

Possible fitness functions include:

- Mean distance from centroid
- Mean distance from all points in a cluster
- Silhouette coefficient

Mean distances from centroid, or from all points in a cluster, are almost baked into algorithms that we will be talking about such as K-Means or EM clustering, but the silhouette coefficient is an interesting take on fitness of cluster mappings.

Silhouette Coefficient

The silhouette coefficient evaluates cluster performance without ground truth (i.e., data that has been provided through direct observation versus inferred observations) by looking at the relation of the average distance inside of a cluster versus the average distance to the nearest cluster (Figure 9-1).

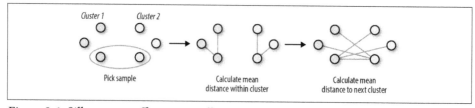

Figure 9-1. Silhouette coefficient visually

Mathematically the metric is:

$$s = \frac{b - a}{max(a, b)}$$

where a is the average distance between a sample and all other points in that cluster and b is the same sample's mean distance to the next nearest cluster points.

This coefficient ends up becoming useful because it will show fitness on a scale of –1 to 1 while not requiring ground truth.

Comparing Results to Ground Truth

In practice many times machine learning involves utilizing ground truth, which is something that we can usually find through trained data sets, humans, or other means like test equipment. This data is valuable in testing our intuition and determining how fitting our model is.

Clustering can be tested using ground truth using the following means:

- Rand index
- Mutual information
- Homogeneity
- Completeness
- V-measure
- Fowlkes-Mallows score

All of these methods can be extremely useful in determining how fit a model is. scikit-learn implements all of these and can easily be used to determine a score.

K-Means Clustering

There are a lot of clustering algorithms like linkage clustering or Diana, but one of the most common is K-Means clustering. Using a predefined K, which is the number of clusters that one wants to split the data into, K-Means will find the most optimal centroids of clusters. One nice property of K-Means clustering is that the clusters will be strict, spherical in nature, and converge to a solution.

In this section we will briefly talk about how K-Means clustering works.

The K-Means Algorithm

The K-Means algorithm starts with a base case. Pick K random points in the data set and define them as centroids. Next, assign each point to a cluster number that is closest to each different centroid. Now we have a clustering based on the original randomized centroid. This is not exactly what we want to end with, so we update where the centroids are using a mean of the data. At that point we repeat until the centroids no longer move (Figure 9-2).

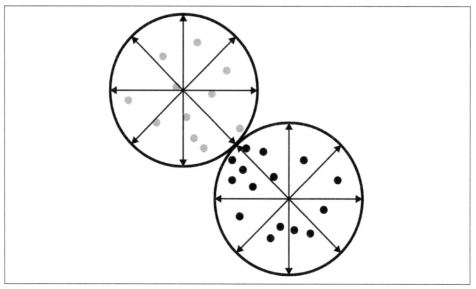

Figure 9-2. In a lot of ways, K-Means resembles a pizza

To construct K-Means clusters we need to have some sort of measurement for distance from the center. Back in Chapter 3 we introduced a few distance metrics, such as:

Manhattan distance

$$d_{manhattan}(x, y) = \Sigma_{i=1}^{n} |x_i - y_i|$$

Euclidean distance

$$d_{euclid}(x, y) = \sqrt{\Sigma_{i=1}^{n} (x_i - y_i)^2}$$

Minkowski distance

$$d(x, y) = \left(\Sigma_{i=1}^{n} |x_i - y_i|^p \right)^{\frac{1}{p}}$$

Mahalanobis distance

$$d(x, y) = \sqrt{\Sigma_{i=1}^{n} \frac{(x_i - y_i)^2}{s_i^2}}$$

For a refresher on the metrics discussed here, review K-Nearest Neighbors in Chapter 3.

Downside of K-Means Clustering

One drawback of this procedure is that everything must have a hard boundary. This means that a data point can only be in one cluster and not straddle the line between two of them. K-Means also prefers spherical data since most of the time the Euclidean distance is being used. When looking at a graphic like Figure 9-3, where the data in the middle could go either direction (to a cluster on the left or right), the downsides become obvious.

EM Clustering

Instead of focusing on finding a centroid and then data points that relate to it, EM clustering focuses on solving a different problem. Let's say that you want to split your data points into either cluster 1 or 2. You want a good guess of whether the data is in either cluster but don't care if there's some fuzziness. Instead of an exact assignment, we really want a probability that the data point is in each cluster.

Another way to think of clustering is how we interpret things like music. Classically speaking, Bach is Baroque music, Mozart is classical, and Brahms is Romantic. Using an algorithm like K-Means would probably work well for classical music, but for more modern music things aren't that simple. For instance, jazz is extremely nuanced. Miles Davis, Sun Ra, and others really don't fit into a categorization. They were a mix of a lot of influences.

So instead of classifying music like jazz we could take a more holistic approach through EM clustering. Imagine we had a simple example where we wanted to classify our jazz collection into either fusion or swing. It's a simplistic model, but we could start out with the assumption that music could be either swing or fusion with a 50% chance. Notating this using math, we could say that $z_k = <0.5, 0.5>$. Then if we were to run a special algorithm to determine what "Bitches Brew—Miles Davis" was in, we might find $z_k = <0.9, 0.1>$ or that it's 90% fusion. Similarly if we were to run this on something like "Oleo—Sonny Rollins" we might find the opposite to be true with 95% being swing.

The beauty of this kind of thinking is that in practice, data doesn't always fit into a category. But how would an algorithm like this work if we were to write it?

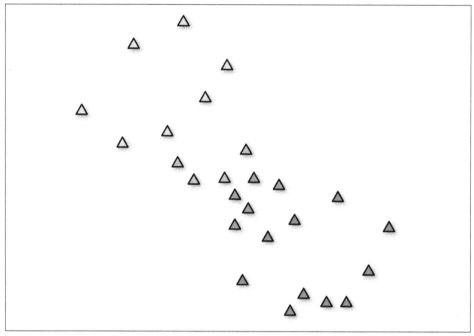

Figure 9-3. This shows how clusters can actually be much softer

Algorithm

The EM clustering algorithm is an iterative process to converge on a cluster mapping. It completes two steps in each iteration: expect and maximize.

But what does that mean? Expectation and maximization could mean a lot.

Expectation

Expectation is about updating the truth of the model and seeing how well we are mapping. In a lot of ways this is a test-driven approach to building clusters—we're figuring out how well our model is tracking the data. Mathematically speaking, we estimate the probability vector for each row of data given its previous value.

On first iteration we just assume that everything is equal (unless you have some domain knowledge you feed into the model). Given that information we calculate the log likelihood of theta in the conditional distribution between our model and the true value of the data. Notated it is:

$$Q(\theta \parallel \theta_t) = E_{Z \parallel X, \theta_t} logL(\theta; X, Z)$$

θ is the probability model we have assigned to rows. Z and X are the distributions for our cluster mappings and the original data points.

Maximization

Just estimating the log likelihood of something doesn't solve our problem of assigning new probabilities to the Z distribution. For that we simply take the argument max of the expectation function. Namely, we are looking for the new θ that will maximize the log likelihood:

$$\theta_t = \text{arg max}_\theta \, Q(\theta \parallel \theta_t)$$

The unfortunate thing about EM clustering is that it does not necessarily converge and can falter when mapping data with singular covariances. We will delve into more of the issues related with EM clustering in "Example: Categorizing Music" on page 170. First we need to talk about one thing that all clustering algorithms share in common: the impossibility theorem.

The Impossibility Theorem

There is no such thing as free lunch and clustering is no exception. The benefit we get out of clustering to magically map data points to particular groupings comes at a cost. This was described by Jon Kleinberg, who touts it as the impossibility theorem, which states that you can never have more than two of the following when clustering:

1. Richness
2. Scale invariance
3. Consistency

Richness is the notion that there exists a distance function that will yield all different types of partitions. What this means intuitively is that a clustering algorithm has the ability to create all types of mappings from data points to cluster assignments.

Scale invariance is simple to understand. Imagine that you were building a rocket ship and started calculating everything in kilometers until your boss said that you need to use miles instead. There wouldn't be a problem switching; you just need to divide by a constant on all your measurements. It is scale invariant. Basically if the numbers are all multiplied by 20, then the same cluster should happen.

Consistency is more subtle. Similar to scale invariance, if we shrank the distance between points inside of a cluster and then expanded them, the cluster should yield the same result. At this point you probably understand that clustering isn't as good as many originally think. It has a lot of issues and consistency is definitely one of those that should be called out.

For our purposes K-Means and EM clustering satisfy richness and scale invariance but not consistency. This fact makes testing clustering just about impossible. The only way we really can test is by anecdote and example, but that is okay for analysis purposes.

In the next section we will analyze jazz music using K-Means and EM clustering.

Example: Categorizing Music

Music has a deep history of recordings and composed pieces. It would take an entire degree and extensive study of musicology just to be able to effectively categorize it all.

The ways we can sort music into categories is endless. Personally I sort my own record collection by artist name, but sometimes artists will perform with one another. On top of that, sometimes we can categorize based on genre. Yet what about the fact that genres are broad—such as jazz, for instance? According to the Montreux Jazz Festival, jazz is anything you can improvise over. How can we effectively build a library of music where we can divide our collection into similar pieces of work?

Instead let's approach this by using K-Means and EM clustering. This would give us a soft clustering of music pieces that we could use to build a taxonomy of music.

In this section we will first determine where we will get our data from and what sort of attributes we can extract, then determine what we can validate upon. We will also discuss why clustering sounds great in theory but in practice doesn't give us much except for clusters.

Setup Notes

All of the code we're using for this example can be found on GitHub (*https:// github.com/thoughtfulml/examples-in-python/tree/master/em-clustering*).

Python is constantly changing so the README is the best place to come up to speed on running the examples.

Gathering the Data

There is a massive amount of data on music from the 1100s through today. We have MP3s, CDs, vinyl records, and written music. Without trying to classify the entire world of music, let's determine a small subsection that we can use. Since I don't want to engage in any copyright suits we will only use public information on albums. This would be Artist, Song Name, Genre (if available), and any other characteristics we can find. To achieve this we have access to a plethora of information contained in Discogs.com. They offer many XML data dumps of records and songs.

Also, since we're not trying to cluster the entire data set of albums in the world, let's just focus on jazz. Most people would agree that jazz is a genre that is hard to really classify into any category. It could be fusion, or it could be steel drums.

To get our data set I downloaded metadata (year, artist, genre, etc.) for the best jazz albums (according to *http://www.scaruffi.com/jazz/best100.html*). The data goes back to 1940 and well into the 2000s. In total I was able to download metadata for about 1,200 unique records. All great albums!

But that isn't enough information. On top of that I annotated the information by using the Discogs API to determine the style of jazz music in each.

After annotating the original data set I found that there are 128 unique styles associated with jazz (at least according to Discogs). They range from aboriginal to vocal.

Coding Design

Although this chapter uses two different algorithms (EM clustering and K-Means clustering), the code will focus on EM clustering and will follow the data flow in Figure 9-4.

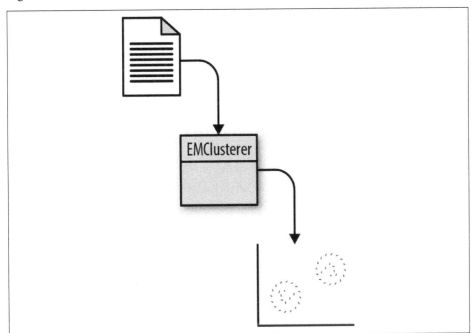

Figure 9-4. EM clustering class

Analyzing the Data with K-Means

Like we did with KNN, we need to figure out an optimal K. Unfortunately with clustering there really isn't much we can test with except to just see whether we split into two different clusters.

But let's say that we want to fit all of our records on a shelf and have 25 slots—similar to the IKEA bookshelf. We could run a clustering of all of our data using K = 25.

```python
import csv

from sklearn.cluster import KMeans

data = []
artists = []
years = []
with open('data/annotated_jazz_albums.csv', 'r') as csvfile:
    reader = csv.DictReader(csvfile)
    headers = reader.fieldnames[3:]
    for row in reader:
        artists.append(row['artist_album'])
        years.append(row['year'])
        data.append([int(row[key]) for key in headers])

clusters = KMeans(n_clusters=25).fit_predict(data)

with open('data/clustered_kmeans.csv', 'w') as csvfile:
    fieldnames = ['artist_album', 'year', 'cluster']
    writer = csv.DictWriter(csvfile, fieldnames=fieldnames)

    writer.writeheader()

    for i, cluster in enumerate(clusters):
        writer.writerow({'artist_album': artists[i],
                'year': years[i],
                'cluster': cluster})
```

That's it! Of course clustering without looking at what this actually tells us is useless. This does split the data into 25 different categories, but what does it all mean?

Looking at a graphic of year versus assigned cluster number yields interesting results (Figure 9-5).

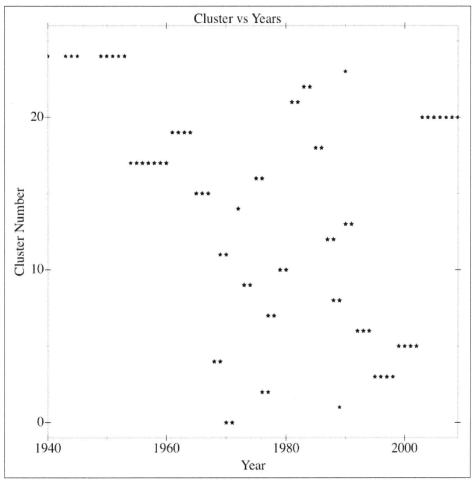

Figure 9-5. K-Means applied to jazz albums

As you can see, jazz starts out in the Big Band era pretty much in the same cluster, transitions into cool jazz, and then around 1959 it starts to go everywhere until about 1990 when things cool down a bit. What's fascinating is how well that syncs up with jazz history.

What happens when we cluster the data using EM clustering?

EM Clustering Our Data

With EM clustering, remember that we are probabilistically assigning to different clusters—it isn't 100% one or the other. This could be highly useful for our purposes since jazz has so much crossover.

Let's go through the process of writing our own code and then use it to map the same data that we have from our jazz data set, then see what happens.

Our first step is to be able to initialize the cluster. If you remember we need to have indicator variables z_t that follow a uniform distribution. These tell us the probability that each data point is in each cluster.

Named Tuples

Tuples in Python are basically immutable arrays. They are fast, and useful when moving data around. But what is a named tuple?

Think of named tuples as lightweight objects that we can use instead of defining a new class. In other languages they might be called structs.

For example, imagine you want to look at points on a Cartesian x,y graph. We could say that a point is basically just (x,y) or we could use a named tuple:

```
from collections import namedtuple

point = (1.0, 5.0)

Point = namedtuple('Point', 'x y')
named_point = Point(1.0, 5.0)

point[0] == named_point.x
point[1] == named_point.y
```

It's more or less syntactic sugar but it can make the code much easier to read with lightweight objects to wrap tuple data in.

Stepping back into our example, we first need to write a helper function that returns the density of a multivariate normal distribution. This is based on how R does this:

```
from collections import namedtuple
import random
import logging
import math

import numpy as np
from numpy.linalg import LinAlgError

def dvmnorm(x, mean, covariance, log=False):
    """density function for the multivariate normal distribution
    based on sources of R library 'mvtnorm'
    :rtype : np.array
    :param x: vector or matrix of quantiles. If x is a matrix, each row is taken
    to be a quantile
    :param mean: mean vector, np.array
    :param covariance: covariance matrix, np.array
```

```
:param log: if True, densities d are given as log(d), default is False
"""
n = covariance.shape[0]
try:
    dec = np.linalg.cholesky(covariance)
except LinAlgError:
    dec = np.linalg.cholesky(covariance + np.eye(covariance.shape[0]) * 0.0001)
tmp = np.linalg.solve(dec, np.transpose(x - mean))
rss = np.sum(tmp * tmp, axis=0)
logretval = -np.sum(np.log(np.diag(dec))) - \
            0.5 * n * np.log(2 * math.pi) - 0.5 * rss
if log:
    return logretval
else:
    return np.exp(logretval)
```

Using all this setup we can now build an `EMClustering` class that will do our EM clustering and log outputs as needed.

This class has the following methods of note:

`partitions`
> Will return the cluster mappings of the data if they are set.

`data`
> Will return the data object passed in.

`labels`
> Will return the membership weights for each cluster.

`clusters`
> Will return the clusters.

`setup`
> This does all of the setup for the EM clustering.

```
class EMClustering(object):
    logger = logging.getLogger(__name__)
    ch = logging.StreamHandler()
    formatstring = '%(asctime)s - %(name)s - %(levelname)s - %(message)s'
    formatter = logging.Formatter(formatstring)
    ch.setFormatter(formatter)
    logger.addHandler(ch)
    logger.setLevel(logging.DEBUG)

    cluster = namedtuple('cluster', 'weight, mean, covariance')

    def __init__(self, n_clusters):
        self._data = None
        self._clusters = None
        self._membership_weights = None
        self._partitions = None
```

```
      self._n_clusters = n_clusters

  @property
  def partitions(self):
    return self._partitions

  @property
  def data(self):
    return self._data

  @property
  def labels(self):
    return self._membership_weights

  @property
  def clusters(self):
    return self._clusters

  def setup(self, data):
    self._n_samples, self._n_features = data.shape
    self._data = data
    self._membership_weights = np.ones((self._n_samples, self._n_clusters)) / \
                              self._n_clusters
    self._s = 0.2

    indices = list(range(data.shape[0]))
    random.shuffle(indices)
    pick_k_random_indices = random.sample(indices, self._n_clusters)

    self._clusters = []
    for cluster_num in range(self._n_clusters):
      mean = data[pick_k_random_indices[cluster_num], :]
      covariance = self._s * np.eye(self._n_features)
      mapping = self.cluster(1.0 / self._n_clusters, mean, covariance)
      self._clusters.append(mapping)

    self._partitions = np.empty(self._n_samples, dtype=np.int32)
```

At this point we have set up all of our base case stuff. We have @k, which is the number of clusters, @data is the data we pass in that we want to cluster, @labels are an array full of the probabilities that the row is in each cluster, and @classes holds on to an array of means and covariances, which tells us where the distribution of data is. Last, @partitions are the assignments of each data row to cluster index.

Now we need to build our expectation step, which is to figure out what the probability of each data row is in each cluster. To do this we need to write a new method, expect, which will do this:

```
class EMClustering(object):
  # __init__
  # setup()
```

```
def expect(self):
  log_likelyhood = 0
  for cluster_num, cluster in enumerate(self._clusters):
    log_density = dvmnorm(self._data, cluster.mean, \
                          cluster.covariance, log=True)
    membership_weights = cluster.weight * np.exp(log_density)
    log_likelyhood += sum(log_density * \
                          self._membership_weights[:, cluster_num])

    self._membership_weights[:, cluster_num] = membership_weights

  for sample_num, probabilities in enumerate(self._membership_weights):
    prob_sum = sum(probabilities)

    self._partitions[sample_num] = np.argmax(probabilities)

    if prob_sum == 0:
      self._membership_weights[sample_num, :] = np.ones_like(probabilities) / \
                                                self._n_clusters
    else:
      self._membership_weights[sample_num, :] = probabilities / prob_sum

  self.logger.debug('log likelyhood %f', log_likelyhood)
```

The first part of this code iterates through all classes, which holds on to the means and covariances of each cluster. From there we want to find the inverse covariance matrix and the determinant of the covariance. For each row we calculate a value that is proportional to the probability that the row is in a cluster. This is:

$$p_{ij} = det(C)e^{-\frac{1}{2}\left(x_j - \mu_i\right)C^{-1}\left(x_j - \mu_i\right)}$$

This is effectively a Gaussian distance metric to help us determine how far outside of the mean our data is.

Let's say that the row vector is exactly the mean. This equation would reduce down to $p_{ij} = det(C)$, which is just the determinant of the covariance matrix. This is actually the highest value you can get out of this function. If for instance the row vector was far away from the mean vector, then p_{ij} would become smaller and smaller due to the exponentiation and negative fraction in the front.

The nice thing is that this is proportional to the Gaussian probability that the row vector is in the mean. Since this is proportional and not equal to, in the last part we end up normalizing to sum up to 1.

Now we can move on to the maximization step:

```
class EMClustering(object):
  # __init__
  # setup()
  # expect

  def maximize(self):
    for cluster_num, cluster in enumerate(self._clusters):
      weights = self._membership_weights[:, cluster_num]
      weight = np.average(weights)
      mean = np.average(self._data, axis=0, weights=weights)
      covariance = np.cov(self._data, rowvar=False, ddof=0, aweights=weights)
      self._clusters[cluster_num] = self.cluster(weight, mean, covariance)
```

Again here we are iterating over the clusters called @classes. We first make an array called sum that holds on to the weighted sum of the data happening. From there we normalize to build a weighted mean. To calculate the covariance matrix we start with a zero matrix that is square and the width of our clusters. Then we iterate through all row vectors and incrementally add on the weighted difference of the row and the mean for each combination of the matrix. Again at this point we normalize and store.

Now we can get down to using this. To do that we add two convenience methods that help in querying the data:

```
class EMClustering(object):
  # __init__
  # setup
  # expect
  # maximize

  def fit_predict(self, data, iteration=5):
    self.setup(data)
    for i in range(iteration):
      self.logger.debug('Iteration %d', i)
      self.expect()
      self.maximize()
    return self
```

The Results from the EM Jazz Clustering

Back to our results of EM clustering with our jazz music. To actually run the analysis we run the following script:

```
import csv

import numpy as np

from em_clustering import EMClustering

np.set_printoptions(threshold=9000)

data = []
```

```
artists = []
years = []

# with open('data/less_covariance_jazz_albums.csv', 'rb') as csvfile:
with open('data/annotated_jazz_albums.csv', 'r') as csvfile:
  reader = csv.DictReader(csvfile)
  headers = reader.fieldnames[3:]
  for row in reader:
    artists.append(row['artist_album'])
    years.append(row['year'])
    data.append([int(row[key]) for key in headers])

clusterer = EMClustering(n_clusters=25)
clusters = clusterer.fit_predict(np.array(data))


print(clusters.partitions)
```

The first thing you'll notice about EM clustering is that it's slow. It's not as quick as calculating new centroids and iterating. It has to calculate covariances and means, which are all inefficient. Ockham's Razor would tell us here that EM clustering is most likely not a good use for clustering big amounts of data.

The other thing that you'll notice is that our annotated jazz music will not work because the covariance matrix of this is singular. This is not a good thing; as a matter of fact this problem is ill suited for EM clustering because of this, so we have to transform it into a different problem altogether.

We do that by collapsing the dimensions into the top two genres by index:

```
import csv

with open('data/less_covariance_jazz_albums.csv', 'w') as csvout:
  writer = csv.writer(csvout, delimiter=',')

  # Write the header of the CSV file
  writer.writerow(['artist_album', 'key_index', 'year', 'Genre_1', 'Genre_2'])

  with open('data/annotated_jazz_albums.csv', 'r') as csvin:
    reader = csv.DictReader(csvin)
    for row in reader:
      genre_count = 0
      genres = [0, 0]
      genre_idx = 0
      idx = 0
      for key, value in row.items():
        break if genre_idx == 2
        if value == '1':
          genres[genre_idx] = idx
          genre_idx += 1
        idx += 1
      if genres[0] > 0 || genres[1] > 0:
        line = [row['artist_album'], row['key_index'], \
```

```
                        row['year'], genres[0], genres[1]]
            writer.writerow(line)
```

Basically what we are doing here is saying for the first two genres, let's assign a genre index to it and store it. We'll skip any albums with zero information assigned to them.

At this point we are able to run the EM clustering algorithm, except that things become too difficult to actually cluster. This is an important lesson with EM clustering. The data we have actually doesn't cluster because the matrix has become too unstable to invert.

Some possibilities for refinement would be to try out K-Means or other clustering algorithms, but really a better approach would be to work on the data some more. Jazz albums are a fun example but data-wise aren't very illustrative. We could, for instance, expand using some more musical genomes, or feed this into some sort of text-based model. Or maybe we could spelunk for musical queues using fast Fourier transforms! The possibilities are really endless but this gives us a good start.

Conclusion

Clustering is useful but can be a bit hard to control since it is unsupervised. Add the fact that we are dealing with the impossibility of having consistency, richness, and scale-invariance all at once and clustering can be a bit useless in many contexts. But don't let that get you down—clustering can be useful for analyzing data sets and splitting data into arbitrary clusters. If you don't care how they are split and just want them split up, then clustering is good. Just know that there are sometimes odd circumstances.

## CHAPTER 10

Improving Models and Data Extraction

How do you go about improving upon a simple machine learning algorithm such as Naive Bayesian Classifiers, SVMs, or really any method? That is what we will delve into in this chapter, by talking about four major ways of improving models:

- Feature selection
- Feature transformation
- Ensemble learning
- Bootstrapping

I'll outline the benefits of each of these methods but in general they reduce entanglement, overcome the curse of dimensionality, and reduce correction cascades and sensitivity to data changes.

They each have certain pros and cons and should be used when there is a purpose behind it. Sometimes problems are so sufficiently complex that tweaking and improvement are warranted at this level, other times they are not. That is a judgment people must make depending on the business context.

Debate Club

I'm not sure if this is common throughout the world, but in the United States, debate club is a high school fixture. For those of you who haven't heard of this, it's a simple idea: high schoolers will take polarizing issues and debate their side. This serves as a great way for students who want to become lawyers to try out their skills arguing for a case.

The fascinating thing about this is just how rigorous and disciplined these kids are. Usually they study all kinds of facts to put together a dossier of important points to make. Sometimes they argue for a side they don't agree with but they do so with conviction.

Why am I telling you this? These debate club skills are the key to making machine learning algorithms (and many cases any algorithm) work better:

- Collecting factual and important data
- Arguing different points of view in multiple ways

As you can imagine, if we could collect *important* or *relevant* data to feed into our models, and try different methods or approaches to the same problem, we will iteratively get better as we find the best model combination.

This gets us into what we will be talking about: picking better data or arguing for solutions more effectively.

Picking Better Data

In this section we'll be discussing how to pick better data. Basically we want to find the most compact, simplest amount of data that backs up what we are trying to solve. Some of that intuitively means that we want the data that supports our conclusion, which is a bit of cart before the horse; regardless, there are two great methods to improve the data one is using: feature selection and feature transformation algorithms.

This sounds like a great idea, but what is the motivation behind picking better data?

Generally speaking, machine learning methods are better suited for smaller dimensions that are well correlated with the data. As we have discussed, data can become extremely overfit, entangled, or track improperly with many dimensions. We don't want to under- or overfit our data, so finding the best set to map is the best use of our time.

Feature Selection

Let's think about some data that doesn't make a whole lot of sense. Say we want to measure weather data and want to be able to predict temperature given three variables: "Matt's Coffee Consumption," "Ice Cream Consumption," and "Season" (see Table 10-1 and Figure 10-1).

Table 10-1. Weather data for Seattle

Average temperature (°F)	Matt's coffee consumption (cups)	Ice cream consumption (scoops)	Month
47	4.1	2	Jan
50	4	2	Feb

Average temperature (°F)	Matt's coffee consumption (cups)	Ice cream consumption (scoops)	Month
54	4	3	Mar
58	4	3	Apr
65	4	3	May
70	4	3	Jun
76	4	4	Jul
76	4	4	Aug
71	4	4	Sep
60	4	3	Oct
51	4	2	Nov
46	4.1	2	Dec

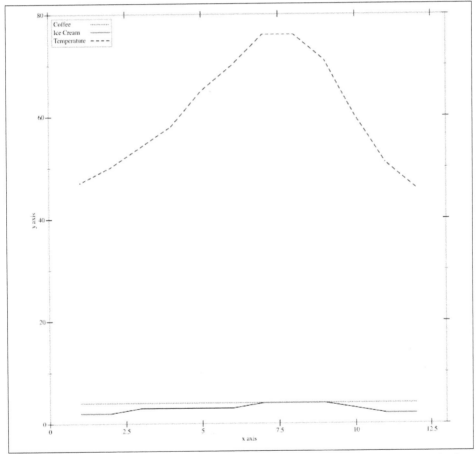

Figure 10-1. A graph comparing my consumption of ice cream (in scoops) and coffee (in cups) with the temperature

Obviously you can see that I generally drink about 4 cups of coffee a day. I tend to eat more ice cream in the summertime and it's generally hotter around that time.

But what can we do with this data? There are at most N choose K solutions to any data set, so given N dimensions, we can find an enormous number of combinations of various-sized subsets.

At this point we want to reduce the amount of dimensions we are looking at but don't know where to start. In general we want to minimize the redundancy of our data while maximizing the relevancy. As you can imagine this is a tradeoff: if we keep all the data, then we'll know 100% that we have relevant data whereas if we reduce some number of dimensions we might have redundancy—especially if we have lots and lots of dimensions.

We have talked about this before as being an entanglement problem with having too many data points that point to the same thing.

In general, redundancy and relevancy are calculated using the same metrics and on a spectrum:

- Correlation
- Mutual information
- Distance from some point (Euclidean distance from reference)

So they actually end up measuring the same thing. How do we solve this?

Let's first take a step back and think about what would happen if we just looked at all possibilities.

Exhaustive Search

Let's imagine that in this case we want to find the best possible dimensions to train on. We could realistically just search through all possibilities. In this case we have three dimensions which would equate to seven models (123, 12, 13, 23, 1, 2, 3). From here we could say that we want to find the model that has the highest accuracy (Figure 10-2).

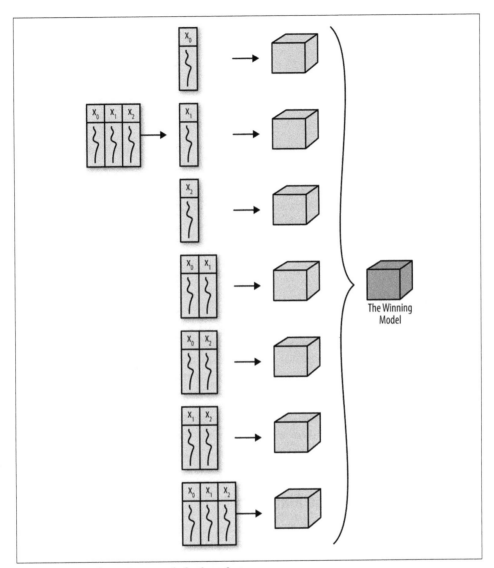

Figure 10-2. Exhaustive search for best features

This unfortunately doesn't work as well as you go up in dimensions. If for instance you have 10 dimensions, the possibilities from selecting 10 dimensions, to 1 dimension would be $2^{10} - 1$. This can be denoted in Pascal's triangle (Figure 10-3) as a sum of combinations where:

$$\binom{10}{10} + \binom{10}{9} + \cdots + \binom{10}{1}$$

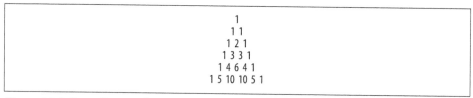

Figure 10-3. Pascal's triangle

Pascal's triangle shows all combinations for a given row. Since each row sums up to 2^n, all we need to do is subtract 1, so we don't account for zero dimensions.

So as you add dimensions you would have to account for $2^n - 1$ possible data sets. If you had 3,000 dimensions (which would be a good reason to use feature selection), you would have roughly a trecentillion (10^{903}) models to run through!

Surely there is a better way. We don't need to try *every* model. Instead, what if we just randomly selected features?

Random Feature Selection

A lot of the time random feature selection will be useful enough for our purposes. Reducing the features by half or a certain amount is an excellent way of improving data overfitting. The added benefit is that you really don't have to think about it much and instead try out a random feature selection of a certain percent.

Say for instance you want to reduce the features by 25%. You could randomly see how it performs for accuracy, precision, or recall. This is a simple way of selecting features, but there is one major downside: what if training the model is slow? You are still brute-forcing your way to finding features. This means that you are arbitrarily picking a number and hoping for the best. Surely there is a better way.

A Better Feature Selection Algorithm

Instead of relying on random feature selection, let's think a little more in terms of what we want to improve with our model. We want to increase relevancy while reducing redundancy. *Relevancy* is a measure of how relevant the dimension in question is versus the classification whereas *redundancy* is a measure of how redundant the dimension is compared to all the other dimensions. Usually for relevancy and redundancy you either use correlation or mutual information.

Correlation is useful for data that is continuous in nature and not nominal. By contrast, mutual information gives us a discrete measure of the mutual information shared between the two dimensions in question.

Using our earlier example, correlation would look like the results in Table 10-2 for relevancy and Table 10-3 for redundancy.

Table 10-2. Relevancy using correlation

Dimension	Correlation to temperature
Matt's coffee consumption	−0.58
Ice cream	0.93
Month	0.16

Table 10-3. Redundancy using correlation

Dimension	Matt's coffee consumption	Ice cream	Month
Matt's coffee consumption	1	−0.54	0
Ice cream	−0.54	1	0.14
Month	0	0.14	1

As you can see from these two tables, ice cream is highly correlated with temperature and my coffee consumption is somewhat negatively correlated with temperature; the month seems irrelevant. Intuitively we would think month would make a huge difference, but since it runs on a modular clock it's hard to model using linear approximations. The redundancy is more interesting. Taken out of context my coffee consumption and month seem to have low redundancy, while coffee and ice cream seem more redundant.

So what can we do with this data? Next I'm going to introduce a significant algorithm that brings this all together.

Minimum Redundancy Maximum Relevance Feature Selection

To bring all of these competing ideas together into one unified algorithm there is minimum redundancy maximum relevance (mRMR) feature selection, which aims to maximize relevancy while minimizing redundancy. We can do this using a maximization (minimization) problem using NumPy and SciPy.

In this formulation we can just minimize the following function:

Equation 10-1. mRMR definition

max *Relevancy* − *Redundancy*

Equation 10-2. Relevancy definition

$$Relevancy = \frac{\Sigma_{i=1}^{n} c_i x_i}{\Sigma_{i=1}^{n} x_i}$$

Equation 10-3. Redundancy definition

$$Redundancy = \frac{\Sigma_{i,j=1}^{n} a_{ij} x_i x_j}{\left(\Sigma_{i=1}^{n} x_i\right)^2}$$

More importantly in code we have:

```
from scipy.optimize import minimize
import numpy as np

matrix = np.array([
  [47, 4.1, 2, 1],
  [50, 4, 2, 2],
  [54,4,3,3],
  [58,4,3,4],
  [65,4,3,5],
  [70,4,3,6],
  [76,4,4,7],
  [76,4,4,8],
  [71,4,4,9],
  [60,4,3,10],
  [51,4,2,11],
  [46,4.1,2,12]
])

corrcoef = np.corrcoef(np.transpose(matrix))
relevancy = np.transpose(corrcoef)[0][1:]

# Set initial to all dimensions on
x0 = [1,1,1]

# Minimize the redundancy minus relevancy

fun = lambda x: sum([corrcoef[i+1, j+1] * x[i] * x[j] for i in range(len(x)) \
                    for j in range(len(x))])/ \
                    (sum(x) ** 2) - \
                    (sum(relevancy * x) / sum(x))

res = minimize(fun, x0, bounds=((0,1), (0,1), (0,1)))

res.x

array([ 0.29820206, 1.       , 0.1621906 ])
```

This gives us almost exactly what we expected: my ice cream consumption models the temperature quite well. For bonus points you could use an integer programming method to get the values to be either 0 or 1, but for these purposes it's obvious which features should be selected to improve the model.

Feature Transformation and Matrix Factorization

We've actually already covered feature transformation quite well in the previous chapters. For instance, clustering and the kernel trick are both feature transformation methods, effectively taking a set of data and projecting it into a new space, whether it's a cluster number or an expanded way of looking at the data. In this section, though, we'll talk about another set of feature transformation algorithms that are rooted in linear algebra. These are generally used to factor a matrix down to a smaller size and generally can be used to improve models.

To understand feature transformation, let's take a look at a few algorithms that transform a matrix into a new, more compressed or more verbose version of itself: principal component analysis and independent component analysis.

Principal Component Analysis

Principal component analysis (PCA) has been around for a long time. This algorithm simply looks at the direction with the most variance and then determines that as the first principal component. This is very similar to how regression works in that it determines the best direction to map data to. Imagine you have a noisy data set that looks like Figure 10-4.

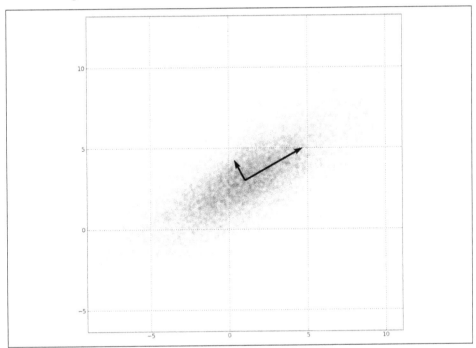

Figure 10-4. Graphical PCA from Gaussian

As you can see, the data has a definite direction: up and to the right. If we were to determine the principal component, it would be that direction because the data is in maximal variance that way. The second principal component would end up being orthogonal to that, and then over iterations we would reduce our dimensions by transforming them into these principal directions.

Another way of thinking about PCA is how it relates to faces. When you apply PCA to a set of faces, an odd result happens known as the Eigenfaces (see Figure 10-5).

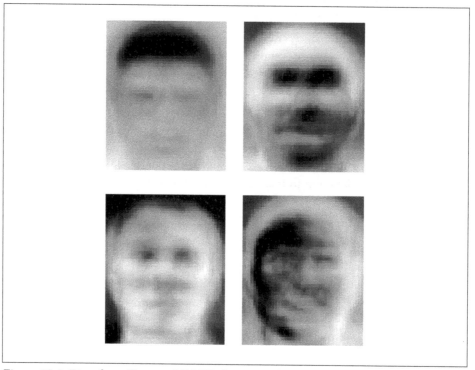

Figure 10-5. Eigenfaces (Source: AT&T Laboratories)

While these look quite odd, it is fascinating that what comes out is really an average face summed up over all of the training data. Instead of implementing PCA now, we'll wait until the next section where we implement an algorithm known as independent component analysis (ICA), which actually relies on PCA as well.

Independent Component Analysis

Imagine you are at a party and your friend is coming over to talk to you. Near you is someone you hate who won't shut up, and on the other side of the room is a washing machine that keeps making noise (see Figure 10-6).

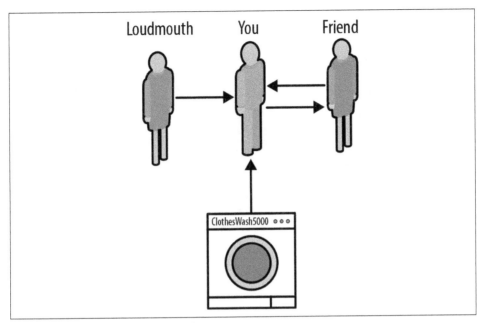

Figure 10-6. Cocktail party example

You want to know what your friend has been up to, so you listen to her closely. Being human, you are adept at separating out sounds like the washing machine and that loudmouth you hate. But how could we do that with data?

Let's say that instead of listening to your friend, you only had a recording and wanted to filter out all of the noise in the background. How would you do something like that? You'd use an algorithm called ICA.

Technically, ICA minimizes mutual information, or the information shared between the two variables. This makes intuitive sense: find me the signals in the aggregate that are different.

Compared to our face recognition example in Figure 10-5, what does ICA extract? Well, unlike Eigenfaces, it extracts features of a face, like noses, eyes, and hair.

PCA and ICA are useful for transforming data and can analyze information even better (see Figure 10-7). Then we can use this more succinct data to feed our models more useful and relevant information, which will improve our models beyond just cross-validation.

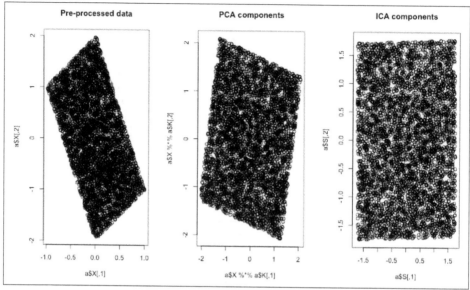

Figure 10-7. ICA extraction example

Now that we know about feature transformation and feature selection, let's discuss what we can do in terms of better arguing for a classiciation or regression point.

Ensemble Learning

Up until this point we have discussed selecting dimensions as well as transforming dimensions into new ones. Both of these approaches can be quite useful when improving models or the data we are using. But there is yet another way of improving our models: ensemble learning.

Ensemble learning is a simple concept: build multiple models and aggregate them together. We have already encountered this with random forests in Chapter 5.

A common example of ensemble learning is actually weather. When you hear a forecast for the next week, you are most likely hearing an aggregation of multiple weather models. For instance, the European model (ECMWF) might predict rain and the US model (GFS) might not. Meterologists take both of these models and determine which one is most likely to hit and deliver that information during the evening news.

When aggregating multiple models, there are two general methods of ensemble learning: *bagging*, a naive method; and *boosting*, a more elegant one.

Bagging

Bagging or bootstrap aggregation has been a very useful technique. The idea is simple: take a training set and generate new training sets off of it.

Let's say we have a training set of data that is 1,000 items long and we split that into 50 training sets of 100 a piece. (Because we sample with replacement, these 50 training sets will overlap, which is okay as long as they are unique.) From here we could feed this into 50 different models.

Now at this point we have 50 different models telling us 50 different answers. Like the weather report just mentioned, we can either find the one we like the most or do something simpler, like average all of them.

This is what bootstrap aggregating does: it averages all of the models to yield the average result off of the same training set. The amazing thing about bagging is that in practice it ends up improving models substantially because it has a tendency to remove some of the outliers.

But should we stop here? Bagging seems like a bit of a lucky trick and also not very elegant. Another ensemble learning tool is even more powerful: boosting.

Boosting

Instead of splitting training data into multiple data models, we can use another method like boosting to optimize the best weighting scheme for a training set.

Given a binary classification model like SVMs, decision trees, Naive Bayesian Classifiers, or others, we can boost the training data to actually improve the results.

Assuming that you have a similar training set to what we just described with 1,000 data points, we usually operate under the premise that all data points are important or that they are of equal importance. Boosting takes the same idea and starts with the assumption that all data points are equal. But we intuitively know that not all training points are the same. What if we were able to optimally weight each input based on what is most relevant?

That is what boosting aims to do. Many algorithms can do boosting but the most popular is AdaBoost.

To use AdaBoost we first need to fix up the training data just a bit. There is a requirement that all training data answers are either 1 or –1. So, for instance, with spam classification we would say that spam is 1 and not spam is –1. Once we have changed our data to reflect that, we can introduce a special error function:

$$E(f(x), y, i) = e^{-y_i f(x_i)}$$

This function is quite interesting. Table 10-4 shows all four cases.

Table 10-4. Error function in all cases

f(x)	y	$e^{-y_i f(x_i)}$
1	1	$\frac{1}{e}$
−1	1	e
1	−1	e
−1	−1	$\frac{1}{e}$

As you can see, when $f(x)$ and y equal, the error rate is minimal, but when they are not the same it is much higher.

From here we can iterate through a number of iterations and descend on a better weighting scheme using this algorithm:

- Choose a hypothesis function (either SVMs, Naive Bayesian Classifiers, or something else)

  — Using that hypothesis, sum up the weights of points that were missclassified:

  $$\epsilon = \Sigma_{h(x) \neq y} w$$

  — Choose a learning rate based on the error rate:

  $$\alpha = \frac{1}{2} ln\left(\frac{1 - \epsilon}{\epsilon}\right)$$

- Add to the ensemble:

  $$F(x) = F_{t-1}(x) + \alpha h_t(x)$$

- Update weights:

  $$w_{i,t+1} = w_{i,t} e^{-y_i \alpha_t h_t(x_i)}$$

  for all weights

- Renormalize weights by making sure they add up to 1

What this does is converge on the best possible weighting scheme for the training data. It can be shown that this is a minimization problem over a convex set of functions.

This meta-heuristic can be excellent at improving results that are mediocre from any weak classifier like Naive Bayesian Classification or others like decision trees.

Conclusion

You've learned a few different tricks of the trade with improving existing models: feature selection, feature transformation, ensemble learning, and bagging. In one big graphic it looks something like Figure 10-8.

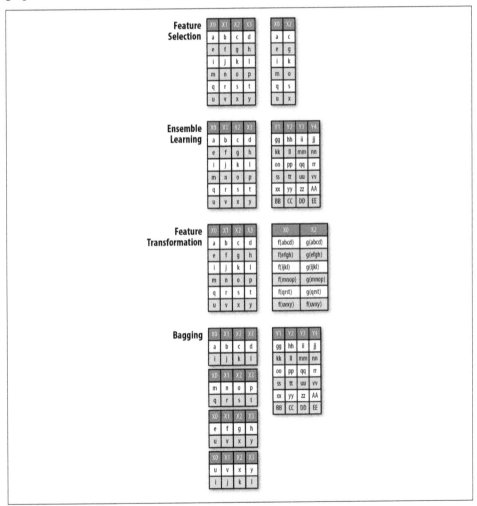

Figure 10-8. Feature improvement in one model

As you can see, ensemble learning and bagging mostly focus on building many models and trying out different ideas, while feature selection and feature transformation are about modifying and studying the training data.

## CHAPTER 11

Putting It Together: Conclusion

Well, here we are! The end of the book. While you probably don't have the same depth of understanding as a PhD in machine learning, I hope you have learned something. Specifically, I hope you've developed a thought process for approaching problems that machine learning works so well at solving. I firmly believe that using tests is the only way that we can effectively use the scientific method. It is the reason the modern world exists, and it helps us become much better at writing code.

Of course, you can't write a test for everything, but it's the mindset that matters. And hopefully you have learned a bit about how you can apply that mindset to machine learning. In this chapter, we will discuss what we covered at a high level, and I'll list some suggested reading so you can dive further into machine learning research.

Machine Learning Algorithms Revisited

As we touched on earlier in the book, machine learning is split into three main categories: supervised, unsupervised, and reinforcement learning (Table 11-1). This book skips reinforcement learning, but I highly suggest you research it now that you have a better background. I'll list a source for you in the final section of this chapter.

Table 11-1. Machine learning categories

Category	Description
Supervised	Supervised learning is the most common machine learning category. This is functional approximation. We are trying to map some data points to some fuzzy function. Optimization-wise, we are trying to fit a function that best approximates the data to use in the future. It is called "supervised" because it has a learning set given to it.
Unsupervised	Unsupervised learning is just analyzing data without any sort of Y to map to. It is called "unsupervised" because the algorithm doesn't know what the output should be and instead has to come up with it itself.

Category	Description
Reinforcement	Reinforcement learning is similar to supervised learning, but with a reward that is generated from each step. For instance, this is like a mouse looking for cheese in a maze. The mouse wants to find the cheese and in most cases will not be rewarded until the end when it finally finds it.

There are generally two types of biases for each of these categories: restriction and preference. Restriction bias is what limits the algorithm, while preference is what sort of problems it prefers.

All of this information (shown in Table 11-2) helps us determine whether we should use each algorithm or not.

Table 11-2. Machine learning algorithm matrix

Algorithm	Type	Class	Restriction bias	Preference bias
K-Nearest Neighbors	Supervised	Instance based	Generally speaking, KNN is good for measuring distance-based approximations; it suffers from the curse of dimensionality	Prefers problems that are distance based
Naive Bayes	Supervised	Probabilistic	Works on problems where the inputs are independent from each other	Prefers problems where the probability will always be greater than zero for each class
Decision Trees/ Random Forests	Supervised	Tree	Becomes less useful on problems with low covariance	Prefers problems with categorical data
Support Vector Machines	Supervised	Decision boundary	Works where there is a definite distinction between two classifications	Prefers binary classification problems
Neural Networks	Supervised	Nonlinear functional approximation	Little restriction bias	Prefers binary inputs
Hidden Markov Models	Supervised/ Unsupervised	Markovian	Generally works well for system information where the Markov assumption holds	Prefers time-series data and memoryless information
Clustering	Unsupervised	Clustering	No restriction	Prefers data that is in groupings given some form of distance (Euclidean, Manhattan, or others)
Feature Selection	Unsupervised	Matrix factorization	No restrictions	Depending on algorithm, can prefer data with high mutual information
Feature Transformation	Unsupervised	Matrix factorization	Must be a nondegenerate matrix	Will work much better on matricies that don't have inversion issues
Bagging	Meta-heuristic	Meta-heuristic	Will work on just about anything	Prefers data that isn't highly variable

How to Use This Information to Solve Problems

Using Table 11-2, we can figure out how to approach a given problem. For instance, if we are trying to determine what neighborhood someone lives in, KNN is a pretty good choice, whereas Naive Bayesian Classification makes absolutely no sense. But Naive Bayesian Classification could determine sentiment or some other type of probability. The SVM algorithm works well for problems such as finding a hard split between two pieces of data, and it doesn't suffer from the curse of dimensionality nearly as much. So SVM tends to be good for word problems where there's a lot of features. Neural networks can solve problems ranging from classifications to driving a car. HMMs can follow musical scores, tag parts of speech, and be used well for other system-like applications.

Clustering is good at grouping data together without any sort of goal. This can be useful for analysis, or just to build a library and store data effectively. Filtering is well suited for overcoming the curse of dimensionality. We saw it used predominantly in Chapter 5 by focusing on important attributes of mushrooms like cap color, smell, and the like.

What we didn't touch on in the book is that these algorithms are just a starting point. The important thing to realize is that it doesn't matter what you pick; it is what you are trying to solve that matters. That is why we cross-validate, and measure precision, recall, and accuracy. Testing and checking our work every step of the way guarantees that we at least approach better answers.

I encourage you to read more about machine learning models and to think about applying tests to them. Most algorithms have them baked in, which is good, but to write code that learns over time, we mere humans need to be checking our own work as well.

What's Next for You?

This is just the beginning of your journey. The machine learning field is rapidly growing every single year. We are learning how to build robotic self-driving cars using deep learning networks, and how to classify health problems. The future is bright for machine learning, and now that you've read this book you are better equipped to learn more about deeper subtopics like reinforcement learning, deep learning, artificial intelligence in general, and more complicated machine learning algorithms.

There is a plethora of information out there for you. Here are a few resources I recommend:

- Peter Flach, *Machine Learning: The Art and Science of Algorithms That Make Sense of Data* (Cambridge, UK: Cambridge University Press, 2012).

- David J. C. MacKay, *Information Theory, Inference, and Learning Algorithms* (Cambridge, UK: Cambridge University Press, 2003).

- Tom Mitchell, *Machine Learning* (New York: McGraw-Hill, 1997).

- Stuart Russell and Peter Norvig, *Artificial Intelligence: A Modern Approach*, 3rd Edition (London: Pearson Education, 2009).

- Toby Segaran, *Programming Collective Intelligence: Building Smart Web 2.0 Applications* (Sebastopol, CA: O'Reilly Media, 2007).

- Richard Sutton and Andrew Barto, *Reinforcement Learning: An Introduction* (Cambridge, MA: MIT Press, 1998).

Now that you know a bit more about machine learning, you can go out and solve problems that are not black and white, but instead involve many shades of gray. Using a test-driven approach, as we have throughout the book, will equip you to see these problems through a scientific lens and to attempt to solve problems not by being true or false but instead by embracing a higher level of accuracy. Machine learning is a fascinating field because it allows you to take two divergent ideas like computer science, which is theoretically sound, and data, which is practically noisy, and zip them together in one beautiful relationship.

Index

About the Author

Matthew Kirk is a data architect, software engineer, and entrepreneur based out of Seattle, WA. For years, he struggled to piece together his quantitative finance background with his passion for building software. Then he discovered his affinity for solving problems with data.

Now, he helps multimillion dollar companies with their data projects. From diamond recommendation engines to marketing automation tools, he loves educating engineering teams about methods to start their big data projects.

To learn more about how you can get started with your big data project (beyond reading this book), check out *matthewkirk.com/tml* for tips.

Colophon

The animal on the cover of *Thoughtful Machine Learning with Python* is the Cuban solenodon (*Solenodon cubanus*), also know as the *almiqui*. The Cuban solenodon is a small mammal found only in the Oriente province of Cuba. They are similar in appearance to members of the more common shrew family, with long snouts, small eyes, and a hairless tail.

The diet of the Cuban solenodon is varied, consisting of insects, fungi, and fruits, but also other small animals, which they incapacitate with venomous saliva. Males and females only meet up to mate, and the male takes no part in raising the young. Cuban solenodons are nocturnal and live in subterranean burrows.

The total number of Cuban solenodons is unknown, as they are rarely seen in the wild. At one point they were considered to be extinct, but they are now classified as endangered. Predation from the mongoose (introduced during Spanish colonization) as well as habitat loss from recent construction have negatively impacted the Cuban solenodon population.

Many of the animals on O'Reilly covers are endangered; all of them are important to the world. To learn more about how you can help, go to *animals.oreilly.com*.

The cover image is from *Lydekker's Royal Natural History*. The cover fonts are URW Typewriter and Guardian Sans. The text font is Adobe Minion Pro; the heading font is Adobe Myriad Condensed; and the code font is Dalton Maag's Ubuntu Mono.

Learn from experts.
Find the answers you need.

Sign up for a **10-day free trial** to get **unlimited access** to all of the content on Safari, including Learning Paths, interactive tutorials, and curated playlists that draw from thousands of ebooks and training videos on a wide range of topics, including data, design, DevOps, management, business—and much more.

Start your free trial at:

oreilly.com/safari

(No credit card required)